Songs of Liberation in the Netherlands

For Jan and Hugo

FRANK MEHRING

Songs of Liberation in the Netherlands

THE TRANSATLANTIC SOUNDTRACK OF FREEDOM

AMSTERDAM UNIVERSITY PRESS

The publication of this book is made possible in part by a gift from the Hugo Keesing and Marilynn Draxl Fund for the Performing Arts.

Cover illustration: Back of the liberation song *Little Holland Girl*.
Words and Music by Dutchie. Luctor, 1945.

Cover design and lay-out: Bart van den Tooren

ISBN 978 90 4857 021 8
e-ISBN 978 90 4857 022 5
DOI 10.5117/9789048570218
NUR 686 | 689

Unless otherwise noted, all images of liberation songs included in this book are sourced from the Keesing Collection at the Freedom Museum. The reproduction of *America hat Rhythmus* is included with the kind permission of the Collection Ludwig Doblinger, photo by Bernhard Herzmansky, KG Wien. Photographs courtesy of the Canadian War Museum Ottawa, Freedom Museum Archive, Muziekschatten Archive, NIOD Institute for War, Holocaust, and Genocide Studies, and Regionaal Archief Nijmegen.

Unless otherwise specified, all translations of song lyrics provided are literal, aiming for accuracy in meaning rather than poetic interpretation or artistic embellishment.

TABLE OF CONTENTS

PRELUDE: FIND THE COST OF FREEDOM IN SONGS 15
(Frank Mehring)

SUITE I: LIBERATION SONGS 25
(Frank Mehring)
1. Sing Your Song of Thanks: *The Soundtrack of Freedom* 32
2. We Did It Before: *Sounding Intercultural Encounters* 38
3. Peace March: *Marching Music between Occupation and Freedom* 44
4. Holland Memories: *Hymns to Freedom and Justice* 53
5. Lili Marleen: *Transatlantic and Transnational War Songs* 57
6. White Stripes in a Sky of Blue: *Fox-Trotting and Flirting* 71
7. I Cannot Swing: *Liberation Boogie-Woogie and Swing* 86
8. Snoezepoes: *Composing and Arranging Liberation Songs* 95
9. Bouncin' in Bavaria: *Broadcasting Dutch Swing in Occupied Germany* 103
10. America, We Thank You: *Consent and Satire* 112
11. As Time Goes By: *Jazz as a Lingua Franca* 117

SUITE II: SOUNDTRACK OF FREEDOM THEN AND NOW 124
1. Playing Liberation Songs: *Interview with Jan Hendriks* 124
(Anja Adriaans and Frank Mehring)
2. Exhibiting Liberation Songs: *The Freedom Museum* 134
(Rense Havinga)
3. Collecting Liberation Songs: *A Transatlantic Quest* 151
(Hugo A. Keesing)
4. Composing Liberation Music: *A Symphony* 159
(Dean Burry)
5. Recording Liberation Songs: *Sonic Bridges* 166
(Frank Mehring)

CONCLUSION 170
(Frank Mehring)

CODA: FOURTEEN LIBERATION SONGS 174
(Jens Barnieck)

POSTLUDE 227
(Jo Riding)

Acknowledgments 230
Notes 232
Bibliography 241
Dutch Liberation Songs 241
American, British and Canadian Songs of War and Liberation 243
Secondary Literature 245
List of Contributors 250
Index of persons 254

I can hardly bear to listen in the kitchen,
since beautiful music stirs me to the very depths of my soul.
Tuesday, April 11, 1944
Anne Frank

Looking back, for me it was as if I
had actually survived the war with music.
December 10, 2014
Jan Hendriks

May the music of liberation
serve as a reminder
of the inspiring heights we can reach
when we continue to strive for
justice, freedom, and democracy.
January 20, 2025
Frank Mehring

Eens komt weer de dag van de vrede, cover (1945)

PRELUDE:
FIND THE COST OF FREEDOM IN SONGS

Frank Mehring

At the height of the Vietnam War in 1970, amidst a world shaken by conflict and yearning for peace, American singer-songwriter Stephen Stills penned one of the most hauntingly beautiful reflections on war and freedom. In just four lines, his song *Find the Cost of Freedom* captured the raw emotions of an era, echoing the fears, hopes, and grief of a generation engulfed in turmoil. The song's enduring resonance is a testament to its timeless message, compelling us to continually reflect on the cost of freedom in the face of violence and war.[1]

Find the cost of freedom
Buried in the ground.
Mother Earth will swallow you.
Lay your body down.

What makes these lines so incredibly moving? They compel us to confront the sobering reality that the freedoms we cherish today have been paid for with the lives of others. The imagery of 'Mother Earth' swallowing the fallen unites us with the countless soldiers and activists who have sacrificed everything for something greater than themselves. The song's true power, however, is fully realized in its musical performance by Crosby, Stills, Nash & Young (CSNY), where the listener becomes an intimate participant in this shared human experience.

The human voice—arguably the most primal and affecting instrument—reaches into the depths of our being, blending rational thought with raw emotion. Each member of CSNY brings a distinct vocal quality to the song: David Crosby's smooth, warm baritone; Stephen Stills' raspy, soulful tenor; Graham Nash's pure, soaring harmonies; and Neil Young's distinctive, nasal timbre that adds a piercing clarity to the blend. Whether performed with a single guitar or a cappella, this song never fails to evoke a powerful emotional response—a mix of reverence for the freedoms we enjoy and, in the best-case scenario, a renewed commitment to safeguarding them.

This sentiment of collective responsibility is reflected in the American civil rights movement, where songs like *We Shall Overcome* performed by Joan Baez and Bob Dylan's anthems like *Blowin' in the Wind*, *The Times They Are A-Changin'*, or *Like a Rolling Stone* united a generation in the fight against war, segregation, and racial injustice. The renowned folk musician and activist Peter Seeger famously reflected on the transformative power of music as a tool for social and political change, arguing that the 'right song at the right time can change history'. In addition, participation was the key for his use of music to bring about change.[2] Music became a rallying cry for equality and a way to channel collective hopes for a world free from oppression.[3] Joan Baez to this day performs the song that once was part of the civil rights movement but has in its DNA the wish for peace across time, nations, and peoples.

We shall live in peace
We shall live in peace
We shall live in peace someday

This book takes us back to a similarly transformative period in history: the final days of World War II. It highlights the period between Operation Market Garden in September 1944 and the jubilant Dutch summer of 1945, when the shadow of war finally lifted. During this brief but significant window, the genre of liberation songs emerged as a powerful expression of newfound freedom. These songs—infused with the joy, relief, and resilience of a people released from tyranny—were much more than mere entertainment. They were declarations of life, victory, and the human spirit's refusal to be subdued.

The surviving sheet music from this era, with its vibrant cover art, witty and poignant lyrics, and often irresistible melodies, offers a rich yet overlooked archive of cultural history. While much has been written about the military strategies, political negotiations, and acts of heroism that shaped the postwar world, the liberation songs provide a unique and deeply personal lens through which to understand this pivotal time.

Exploring the cost of freedom through art—especially music—offers us a deeply engaging opportunity to appreciate the lives we lead in democratic societies and reminds us of our duty to preserve the values we hold dear. In his book *Noise: The Political Economy of Music*, the French theorist Jacques Attali argued that music often foretells social and political change. He suggested that shifts in musical styles and practices can act as early indicators of broader societal transformations. Conversely, music can also be a tool for those in power to maintain control, propagating official ideologies and suppressing dissent. Yet, when wielded by the oppressed, music becomes a form of resistance—to mobilize, inspire, and bring about change. Liberation songs are quintessential examples of this, functioning as powerful weapons against tyranny.

Just as the civil rights movement used music to unite and inspire people in their struggle for equality and justice, this tradition of resistance through music has transcended time and borders. Decades later, in a vastly different context, the Russian punk collective Pussy Riot carried forward this legacy, using their performances to confront authoritarianism and demand accountability. While the movements differ in their historical and cultural circumstances, both demonstrate the enduring power of music as a rallying force for freedom and social change.

While Attali's analysis emphasizes music as both a forecaster of social change and a tool for maintaining power, the performances of the Russian Punk group Pussy Riot serve as a potent example of how music can be harnessed by the oppressed to resist authoritarianism. By fusing art with activism, Pussy Riot directly challenges the structures of control that Attali suggests music can help dismantle, reinforcing the idea that music is not only a reflection of societal shifts but also an active agent in the fight for freedom. Their performance of the punk prayer *Virgin Mary, Mother of God, Drive Putin Away* inside Moscow's Cathedral of Christ the Savior in 2012 exemplified their defiance, using provocative lyrics and location to criticize the close relationship between church and state. The song title encapsulates the core of the protest, calling for divine intervention to remove Putin from power. Other parts of the lyrics such as 'The Church's praise of rotten leaders!' criticize the Russian Orthodox Church for supporting Putin and aligning with corrupt political leadership or 'Black robes, golden epaulettes; Freedom's phantom's gone to heaven!' metaphorically reference the clergy's opulence and their abandonment of the ideals of freedom. Music, in this context, transcends entertainment, becoming a vehicle for political resistance, catalyzing public discourse, and embodying a collective yearning for freedom.[4]

The tradition of using music to celebrate freedom and as a call to action whenever liberty is threatened continues to thrive in today's global cultural environment. Modern anthems like Lady Gaga's *Born This Way* and Katy Perry's *Roar* echo the same themes of self-expression and liberation from societal constraints. In Nate Parker's 2016 film *Birth of a Nation*, the protagonist's call to 'Sing to him a new song!' is powerfully underscored by Andra Day's soulful *Rise Up*, a song that has become a modern hymn for justice and equality.

I'll rise up
Rise like the day
I'll rise up
In spite of the ache
I will rise a thousand times again
And we'll rise up
High like the waves
We'll rise up
In spite of the ache
We'll rise up
And we'll do it a thousand times again.

The combination of this soulful hymn to unite and rise up, along with an angry group of African American slaves armed with weapons running toward the camera—and thus the viewers—willing to sacrifice their lives for the cause of freedom, creates one of the most powerful sequences in recent film history.[5] The cost of freedom is measured, in part, by the countless crosses that stand as silent tributes to the sacrifices of those who fought for it.

The Dutch liberation song *Zij, die vielen..!*, with lyrics by Anton Beuving and music by Tom Erich—who also collaborated on other liberation songs like *Vrijheid en Recht* and *Herrijzend Nederland*—speaks about the many crosses in the Netherlands honoring international soldiers who died for Dutch freedom so that Dutch citizens and their European allies could live in peace. While the title refers to 'those who fell', the lyrics focus not on nationality, but on remembering all who died for freedom during the war. The chorus encourages everybody to take note, be humble and grateful for the freedom that is so precious in light of all the pain and sacrifice of human lives:

> Wil bij dat kruis dan even knielen,
> Strooi eens wat bloemen op het graf
> Eert hen, die voor jouw vrijheid vielen,
> Neem even daar je hoed voor af ....
>
> Kneel then at that cross for a moment,
> Scatter some flowers on the grave
> Honor those who fell for your freedom,
> Take your hat off to them ....

By looking at and listening to the rich musical heritage of liberation songs, we gain a deeper appreciation of the resilience and joy that define the human spirit in times of war and liberation. This book not only revisits a pivotal historical moment but also connects it to broader themes of freedom and democracy in the new millennium, at a time that war in the Middle East and Ukraine informs our everyday approach to reevaluating the cost of freedom.

Liberation songs—past and present—serve as powerful reminders of the continuous effort required to uphold and cherish the values of a free society. Ultimately, this book is a call to engage with our history, to search, to question, and to understand the true cost of freedom via the medium of music. It is also a call to defend and cherish the value of freedom.

My work on liberation songs offers a comprehensive exploration of the musical landscape shaped by the events of World War II and its aftermath, with a particular focus on the liberation period of 1944-45. The book examines how music both reflected and influenced the sentiments of freedom, resistance, and cultural exchange during and after the war. Divided into distinct sections, it reveals the complex role music played in helping people make sense of their newfound freedom.

Songs of Liberation is structured into two main sections, Suite I and Suite II. I use the term 'suite' metaphorically to describe a series of chapters that are thematically linked, similar to how movements in a musical suite are connected. Each chapter or section within a 'suite' explores a different aspect of the broader theme, contributing to a comprehensive understanding of the subject. Suite I, titled 'Liberation Songs', explores various dimensions of music. It begins with 'Sing Your Song of Thanks', which examines the 'soundtrack of freedom' and how songs of gratitude permeated the postwar era. The subsequent chapters, such as 'We Did It Before' and 'Peace March', explore the intercultural exchanges and the role of marching music in shaping both occupation and liberation narratives. Other chapters like 'Lili Marleen' and 'White Stripes in a Sky of Blue' investigate the transnational and transatlantic influences on wartime songs, showing how they became part of a shared cultural heritage. Suite I concludes with an analysis of the evolution of musical genres like swing and jazz in 'As Time Goes By', highlighting their role as a lingua franca in the postwar period.[6]

Suite II, titled 'Soundtrack of Freedom Then and Now', presents contributions from five distinct voices: a researcher, a musician from the liberation era, a museum curator, a sheet music collector, and a contemporary composer of liberation. Together, they offer diverse perspectives on liberation songs, drawing from various disciplines and spanning countries like the Netherlands, Germany, the United States, and Canada. Thus, the second suite shifts focus to contemporary reflections on liberation songs. It includes an interview by Anja Adriaans and myself with Jan Hendriks on performing the liberation songs today. In this interview on 'Playing Liberation Songs', Hendriks recounts his experiences as a young musician during

Score of *Zij, die vielen..!* (1945)

World War II and the immediate post-liberation period in the Netherlands. Hendriks, initially a classical piano student, became captivated by jazz after discovering Duke Ellington records. This music, which was considered scandalous at the time, became a significant part of his life, contrasting sharply with the conservative and religious Dutch society. During the war, Hendriks and his friends played jazz in private gatherings due to the restrictions on public activities. After the liberation, he performed regularly for Allied troops, reflecting on the complex mix of freedom, fear, and the surreal atmosphere in the city of Nijmegen. Despite the dangers, music provided an outlet and a sense of liberation for Hendriks and others.

In 'Collecting Liberation Songs', Hugo A. Keesing recounts his dedication to collecting and preserving World War II-era music from the Netherlands. He highlights the significance of this largely overlooked cultural heritage. Despite the publication of over 350 pieces of sheet music between

Cover of *Zij, die vielen..!* (1945)

1938 and 1948, only a fraction were formally recorded. Keesing, driven by a family history of collecting and a personal connection to the war, amassed a significant collection of these songs. His dedication led to the donation of over 300 pieces to the Freedom Museum in the Netherlands in 2012, where they were cataloged, digitized, and displayed. This collection has since become a vital part of understanding the cultural impact of the war, especially through local efforts to revive these songs via concerts and recordings, transforming them into a living soundtrack of Holland's liberation.

'Exhibiting Liberation Songs' by archivist Rense Havinga explores the pivotal role of music during World War II as both a propaganda tool and an emotional outlet. The chapter focuses on how music reflected and influenced societal attitudes, particularly through the relationships between Allied soldiers and Dutch women during and after the liberation of the Netherlands. Songs from this period, like those found in the Keesing Collection, reveal the shifting public opinion—from initial euphoria and romanticism to eventual disillusionment and criticism. Havinga argues that music, often overlooked in historical research and exhibitions, offers a unique and valuable perspective of historical events. By incorporating music into museum exhibits, historians can engage audiences more deeply, conveying the emotions and experiences of the time in a way that traditional archival sources cannot.

Composer Dean Burry reflects on what it means to compose a soundtrack of freedom and liberation from a Canadian perspective in today's world. In his contribution, Burry connects the liberation songs of 1944 and 1945 with the visual narrative of embedded war artist Alex Colville. He draws inspiration from these historical elements to bring the sounds of the past into the present, commemorating 80 years of liberation through music. Burry's work emphasizes the connection between art, music, and the human experience, particularly in the context of war. Drawing on his extensive research and personal experiences at the sites Colville painted, Burry composed the symphonic tone poem *Tracing Colville*. The work premiered with the Kingston Symphony Orchestra in 2022 and was performed in 2024 at a concert in Nijmegen commemorating the 80th anniversary of liberation.[7] The work is divided into four movements, each reflecting on a different aspect of Colville's war experiences. Through this composition, Burry not only honors the history of liberation but also explores the enduring impact of war on both art and society. His approach bridges the past and present, offering a sonic reminder of the sacrifices made and the resilience of the human spirit.

Finally, the 'Coda' showcases fourteen Dutch liberation songs collected by Hugo Keesing, with introductions by pianist Jens Barnieck. These songs capture the emotions and spirit of the Dutch people during their liberation, now brought to life through newly recorded performances available on the Canadian Tulip Festival's website. Many songs had never been recorded before, making this collection a significant preservation of cultural heritage. The recordings feature artists from both sides of the Dutch–German border, performed at venues like Radboud University and the Freedom Museum during commemorations of World War II events. This project underscores the profound impact of experiencing music through performance and expresses gratitude to all participants who help inspire future generations with the enduring spirit of freedom and mutual understanding.

Through this book, I invite readers to explore the rich cultural resource of liberation songs—images, music, texts, and contexts—that not only recount historical events but also reveal their lasting influence on cultural memory and the complex role of music to shed light on a specific historical period.

SUITE I: LIBERATION SONGS

Frank Mehring

Photographs of victory and liberation from 1945 have etched themselves into the collective memory of contemporary viewers. In the United States, iconic images like the snapshot of a jubilant sailor kissing a nurse in Times Square on V-J Day immediately come to mind. Equally memorable are the scenes of the liberation of Paris, with crowds of French patriots lining the Champs Élysées as Allied tanks and half-tracks pass through the Arc de Triomphe on August 25, 1944. Other powerful images include the Soviet flag being raised over the Berlin Reichstag during the Battle of Berlin on May 2, 1945, the liberation of concentration camps like Mauthausen, Dachau, and Buchenwald by the U.S. Third Army in April 1945, and photos of civilians joyfully greeting homecoming soldiers and Allied liberators.

In the Netherlands, one of the most popular images of the liberation is of a Canadian Seaforth Highlander on a motorbike with two laughing girls on the backseat on Amstellaan in Amsterdam (later renamed Vrijheidslaan, or Freedom Lane). These scenes have become central to the Dutch collective memory of the liberation, frequently appearing in newspapers, magazines, documentaries, feature films, social media platforms, and countless websites.

Recently, I came across a remarkable image from my new hometown, Nijmegen, which was liberated during Operation Market Garden in September 1944. This photograph captures a crowd gathered in front of a large brick building, singing, and dancing. It was taken the following year on the memorable May 5, when the liberation of the Netherlands became official. This image, like so many others, invites us to explore the deeper story behind the visual documentation of liberation and the soundtrack that accompanied these historic moments.[8]

The feeling of newfound freedom bursts forth in seemingly spontaneous, improvised performances. A piano, dragged from a nearby house, stands proudly in front of the Nutsschool at Hertogplein. The piano player sings and flirts with a woman beside him, while children perch in a church alcove slightly above, observing the lively scene. At the intersection of Gerard Noodtstraat and Van der Brugghenstraat in downtown Nijmegen, young men and women dance with each other, celebrating the end of the war. This scene captures gratitude for liberation from occupation and a vital way to cope with the surrounding loss and destruction.[9] Yet the image remains silent. What kind of soundtrack accompanies this scene? Could it be a popular Duke Ellington number? One of the latest swing tunes, jive, foxtrot, or jitterbug hits? Or perhaps something entirely different, something that defies expectation?

The questions linger, inviting us to imagine the rhythms and melodies that filled the air on that unforgettable day.

The Freedom Museum in Groesbeek captures the essence of liberation and the exhilaration of newfound freedom in the concluding section of its exhibition. One of the standout pieces is an original drum set, which was played in the streets around Nijmegen and in bars to beat out the rhythm of freedom. This powerful symbol echoes the spirit of celebration and unity that followed liberation, much like the iconic songs of folk group Peter, Paul and Mary that spread messages of hope and freedom among the people. Through this dynamic display, the museum vividly portrays how music became a vital force in amplifying the joy of freedom during this pivotal moment in history.

People dancing on Liberation Day on Hertogplein in front of the local school (Nutsschool) between Gerard Noodtstraat and Van der Brugghenstraat on May 5, 1945. Fotocollectie Regionaal Archief Nijmegen. Detail

If I had a hammer
I'd hammer in the morning
I'd hammer in the evening
All over this land
I'd hammer out danger
I'd hammer out a warning
I'd hammer out love between my brothers and my sisters
All over this land.

We can vividly imagine the overwhelming joy and the powerful pulse of freedom that reverberated across the Netherlands during liberation. The sounds of celebration, symbolized by the beating of drums, echoed through the streets, marking the nation's newfound liberty. Complementing this auditory celebration, the museum presents a striking visual counterpart: the national liberation skirts. These skirts, crafted from repurposed materials, became symbols of the emotional transformation taking place. The patches of worn fabric stitched onto each skirt told a personal story of the war—each one unique, each one a testament to individual experience.

For Dutch women, these skirts served as a kind of uniform, worn proudly during liberation parades. They were not just garments but statements of resilience and identity. According to the museum's narrative, they contributed to 'a Dutch sense of unity', highlighting the role women played in both the war effort and the liberation. The skirts offered a way for women to express their evolving role in society, symbolizing their participation in and contribution to the nation's newfound freedom. The skirt presented at the center has a powerful and resounding message stitched across the diagonal orange rectangular square: 'Thanks to our Liberators!'

Meanwhile, the combination of the rhythmic drums and the vibrant skirts hinted at the profound way music and movement infused the joyous dances and celebrations that followed. But one can only wonder—what did the sounds of freedom truly feel like? What music filled the air as people danced and embraced their long-awaited liberation?

Liberation Drums and Liberation Skirts at the Freedom Museum in Groesbeek. © F. Mehring

Historians have been surprisingly silent about the sounds and soundtrack of history. In retrospect, the signature sound for the Dutch liberation has become American jazz, particularly swing music, crooners like Bing Crosby, Jimmy Dorsey, or Frank Sinatra, female stars including Vera Lynn, Dinah Shore, Doris Day, and the close harmonies of The Andrews Sisters. This is evident in today's annual performances on May 5th (Liberation Day) in major cities like Amsterdam, Arnhem, The Hague, Nijmegen, Rotterdam, and Utrecht with musical tunes and songs like *Chattanooga Choo-Choo*, *Don't Sit under the Apple Tree (With Anyone Else but Me)*, *G.I. Jive*, *Rum and Coca-Cola*, *We'll Meet Again*, *Sentimental Journey*, *That Old Black Magic*, *There's a Star-Spangled Banner Waving Somewhere*, or *(I've Got a Gal in) Kalamazoo*.

Much of the original documentary film material about the liberation, however, is silent. In most cases, we do not have authentic audio recordings to accompany those familiar images of people singing and dancing—images that have been endlessly recycled in documentaries and news clips about the liberation. Instead, a commentator and prerecorded music are often added in postproduction. Most often, this music is linked to jazz and swing, featuring the sound of American big bands. A paradigmatic example is the film trailers where scenes of cheering Dutch citizens and Allied liberators celebrating in public spaces are underscored with music. Often, the scenes are accompanied with the cheerful and exciting swing music of Glenn Miller's famous composition *In the Mood* (1939). This link between liberation and jazz has become so popular that by now it resembles a cliché. The cover reflects this promise with Glenn Miller appearing like a new star on the nightly sky in front of a new moon rising.

To truly understand the soundtrack of liberation as it was heard on the streets in 1945, we must delve into the history of media—the quirks, practices, and limitations of the time. Only then can we begin to piece together the authentic sounds that echoed through those momentous days.

With an abundance of recordings available to fill the silent images of Europe's liberation, American jazz music often becomes a compelling addition to these historic clips. The influence of American culture, or what some scholars refer to as a 'reference culture', goes beyond mere entertainment—it's a potent blend of political, economic, and cultural power. This 'soft power' of cultural appeal plays a crucial role in how certain nations set guiding standards for others.

But this raises an intriguing question: Why do we so often associate the soundtrack of Europe's liberation with American music? What other musical narratives might have accompanied the liberation in the streets and squares of Dutch cities? Could it be that the true history of liberation's soundtrack is yet to be fully uncovered?

Music, as a medium, has a unique ability to cross cultural, ethnic, racial, and national boundaries.[10] Critics like Wilfried Raussert and Reinhold Wagnleitner argue that music, more than any other form of expression, travels effortlessly across borders, creating new cultural contact zones.[11] During and after the Allied liberation of Europe, popular music and jazz became powerful symbols of new beginnings, establishing a shared lingua franca that continues to shape our cultural memory. Philosopher Jacques Attali suggests that music is 'a way of perceiving the world' and 'a tool of understanding'.[12] Building on this idea, I will explore how music transformed the imagery of destruction, despair, and hope into a new emotional landscape.

How can we critically analyze, map, and evaluate the connections between sights, sites, and sounds of memory? How can we trace the processes of cultural flows, as William Uricchio discusses,[13] and the (re)mediation of these experiences, following Jay David Bolter and Richard Grusin?[14] To what extent does our cultural memory of music differ from the experiential memory—the actual sounds and songs performed and heard in 1945, as Aleida Assmann describes?

My aim is to offer a triangular perspective of the songs of liberation, combining insights from the United States (as a reference culture) with those from the neighboring countries of the Netherlands and Germany. This approach will help analyze moments of cultural contact, transfer, and the often contested memories of liberation. The soundtrack of liberation, encoded in what is known as liberation sheet music—with its elaborate cover designs, multilingual lyrics, and references to new dances—provides a new lens through which to examine the politics and cultures of liberation from a performative perspective.

Glenn Miller, *In the Mood*, 1939

1
SING YOUR SONG OF THANKS: THE SOUNDTRACK OF FREEDOM

In 1942, literary critic and writer Samuel Sillen made a compelling argument for using music as a weapon against the Axis powers: 'We need songs, not corn. Songs that make us burn with hatred against the Fascist enemy. Songs that make us cheer the heroism of our armed forces. Songs of dignity, hope, and courage. Fighting songs that rouse and rally.'[15] During World War II, the American music industry aligned itself with the war effort, producing anthems of patriotism and resistance. Following the Allied victory, the European Recovery Program, also known as the Marshall Plan, harnessed all channels of communication, including music, to convey the value of freedom and the benefits of economic aid to European citizens.[16]

The Netherlands offers a particularly intriguing case to examine the impact of what I call transatlantic sonic diplomacy. How did music shape the Dutch memory of liberation and economic recovery? This book explores the soft power of music in the 1940s and delves into how Dutch liberation songs navigated the complex emotions of attraction and repulsion towards the Allied liberators.

With the archive of sheet music, we can begin to reconstruct the soundtrack of liberation. The term 'soundtrack' is typically associated with film, encompassing spoken language, musical compositions, and sound effects. Soundscape theoretician R. Murray Schafer describes 'sound' as the 'sonic universe'[17]—the totality of sounds produced by anyone or anything. However, my focus is on an exclusive rather than an inclusive definition of music.[18]

While the influential avant-garde composer John Cage argued that our traditional conception of music is too narrow and that 'music is sounds, sounds around us whether we're in or out of concert halls',[19] I am interested in the specific songs and musical performances that emerged at the end of the war and during the 'magical summer of liberation' in 1945. But how can we determine what kind of music was actually played and heard at the time of liberation?

The unique collection of sheet music in the archive of the Freedom Museum in Groesbeek provides a key to the soundtrack of the otherwise silent photos depicting dancing people in the spring and summer of 1945.

Hugo Keesing played a crucial role in the rediscovery of liberation songs. Keesing, a retired adjunct associate professor of Psychology and American Studies at the University of Maryland, donated his collection of Dutch sheet music, which reflects various aspects of the liberation experience. Born in The Hague, Keesing emigrated to the United States with his parents in 1951. He developed an interest in the political function of music during the Vietnam War as well as World War II. His 1972 dissertation, *Youth in Transition: A Content Analysis of Two Decades of Popular Music*, is an early example of critical academic analysis of popular music. At that time, such music was often dismissed as an 'unpleasant manifestation of youthful rebellion, including a lack of good musical taste, which most teenagers would inevitably outgrow'.[20]

There are approximately 350 pieces of sheet music that thematize the Dutch experience of war and liberation between 1938 and 1948. Of these compositions, fewer than 50 were officially recorded. Keesing explains that 30 titles address the prewar mobilization period and about twice as many address aspects of the occupation. Around 160 titles can be categorized as liberation songs, while another 40 focus on the postwar reconstruction period.[21]

The sheet music collection reminds us that liberation songs enjoyed particular popularity at the end of the Second World War in the Netherlands. For the most part, this cultural phenomenon has so far remained under the radar of musicologists and cultural historians.[22] A photo of an advertisement in the front window of an Amsterdam music shop suggests that liberation songs were in high demand in 1945. Underneath the headline 'Bevrijdingsliederen' in capital letters, the expression 'alhier verkrijgbaar' ['available here'] with a large exclamation mark (most likely in the color orange; alas, the photo is in black and white) indicates a sense of urgency and desire: Yes, we do have liberation songs available here! The collection offers a fascinating opportunity to explore, describe, and hear the soundtrack of liberation. With these musical notes and lyrics captured on paper, we may get closer to answering the question of what kind of music was played, what kind of songs were sung, and what kind of dances were performed in the summer of 1945. Surprisingly, apart from exceptions like *Trees heeft een Canadees*, *Als op het Leidseplein de lichtjes weer eens branden gaan*, or *Lili Marleen*, few people remember songs like *Vrij is Nederland*, *V-E Day*, *Herrijzend Nederland*, *Da-ag, Da-ag, Da-ag (How I like this way to say 'Hello')*,

Rotterdam Ahoy, *Rotterdams Glorie*, *Little Holland Girl*, *Eens zal de Wereld Zingen*, *Rood Wit Blauw*, *The Tommy Song*, *Goodbye Tommie*, *Tulips Bloom in Holland Once Again*, *Weet je Wat een Zoentje is? Een Zoentje is 'A Little Kiss'*, or *De 'Sten-Gun Walk'.* This remarkable gap in the history of Dutch liberation music begs for an explanation. Why have most of these songs, which formed the soundtrack of liberation, been largely forgotten? This book seeks to uncover the answers, bringing to light a vital but overlooked aspect of the Dutch experience during and after World War II.[23]

Before taking a close look the scores, it is essential to establish the foundation of my project on the 'soundtrack of liberation' and define its terms. Since the nineteenth-century lantern shows and the emergence of film in the 1890s, music has served to heighten emotional impact and bridge the gap between the technical projection of a fictitious world and the illusion of reality. However, the intersection of liberation, music, and songs extends far beyond this era. It reaches back to ancient times, finding prominence in the oldest parts of the Bible.[24]

For instance, in the biblical narrative, when God led the Israelites through the desert, parted the sea, and guided them with a fire in the sky towards

Photo by Boris Kowadlo. Advertisement of liberation songs in a music store shop window in Amsterdam (1945). Netherlands Photo Museum, Rotterdam

the land of freedom—Israel—Moses sang the song of liberation and deliverance: 'Then sang Moses and the children of Israel this song unto the LORD, and spake, saying, I will sing unto the LORD, for he hath triumphed gloriously: the horse and his rider hath he thrown into the sea. The LORD is my strength and song, and he is become my salvation' (Exodus 2, Chapter 15, King James Version).

Advertisement for Kees Manders' repertoire of Liberation Songs: *Zie ginds komt de Stoomboot, Ondergedoken, Wie helpt zwarthandelaar, Heb gezucht jaar in Vught, werd gelucht toen gevlucht, Een NSB-er zonder hoop, In naam van Oranje, Het tankie.* Regionaal Archief Nijmegen

To comprehend the role of music within the sociocultural and political dynamics of oppression and liberation, it's imperative to consider the various functions that Attali attributed to music. Firstly, in a ritualistic context, it has the power to 'make people forget', particularly the trauma of extreme violence. Secondly, in a commercial realm, it can 'instill belief in the harmony of the world'. Thirdly, within the framework of capitalism and mass production, it can be utilized to silence and censor.[25] When examining the concrete manifestation of film music, Siegfried Kracauer's insights are invaluable. He contended that music provides a 'meaningful continuity in time', aiding the audience in perceiving 'structural patterns where there were none before'.[26] This observation holds particular significance when considering the impact of music on the perception of liberation.

Music also acts as a unifying force amid the potentially disjointed visual elements of film—such as various shots, angles, narratives, and jump cuts. A soundtrack can compensate for these visual disruptions. In his seminal work, *The Aesthetics and Psychology of Cinema*, the influential French film theorist Jean Mitry explores the connection between visual disruption and the mind's capacity to establish new continuities. Music plays a pivotal role in this process: 'It is all too apparent that the editing of a series of fixed shots establishes a feeling of continuity but is unable, unlike moving shots, to create the sensation of the continuous, since this sensation is reconstructed intellectually and not perceived as such—which means that reality appears as though it were an idea or memory; or, to put it another way, it appears restructured'.[27] In other words, music helps restructure memory, enabling us to weave together a coherent narrative from fragmented experiences like war, destruction, camaraderie, international encounters, and liberation.

In the context of liberation music, I propose to distinguish between four distinct types:

1. **Liberation songs**: These have a rich history, often originating in oral tradition before being committed to writing. They've shaped the cultural fabric of the Western world through mediums like the Bible and poetry, and their influence extends to more recent examples from the transatlantic world. This includes poetry from pivotal moments such as the American Revolutionary War, the French Revolution, the German Wars of Liberation, and both World Wars. Throughout history, poems from earlier periods have resurfaced as songs in later conflicts, demonstrating their enduring relevance and power. For instance, Theodor Körner's patriotic poetry from the German Wars of Liberation found new life as songs during World War I, while Walt Whitman's works from the American Civil War were rediscovered and repurposed during World War II.
2. **Musical soundtracks**: These have been integral to the cinematic depiction of war and liberation. Even before the advent of sound film, classical music was often used to frame sequences of 'liberation', such as Wagner's 'Ride of the Valkyries' in D.W. Griffith's *Birth of a Nation* (1915). From the end of World War II to the present day, musical scores have played a pivotal role in enhancing the wartime and liberation experiences depicted in films. Composers like Gail Kubik (*The Memphis Belle*, 1944), Hugo Friedhofer (*The Best Years of Our Lives*, 1946), Victor Young (*Sands of Iwo Jima*, 1949), Jerry Goldsmith (*Patton*, 1970), John Williams (*Saving Private Ryan*, 1996), Alexandre Desplat (*The Monuments Men*, 2014), and Volker Bertelmann (*All Quiet on the Western Front*, 2022) have crafted evocative soundscapes that deeply resonate with audiences.

3. **Concert music**: Composed for sociocultural and politically significant moments, concert music has captured the essence of pivotal events throughout history. From the American Revolution to the French Revolution, from the German Wars of Liberation to both World Wars, and from the Vietnam War to the fall of the Berlin Wall in 1989 and the subsequent newfound freedom of Eastern European countries, composers have been inspired to reflect these significant events in their music. In the final period of World War II and the early postwar years, notable compositions include works like Arturo Toscanini's *Hymn of the Nations*, Dmitri Shostakovich's *United Nations on the March* (featured in the MGM wartime musical *Thousands Cheer* from 1943, with a symphonic transcription by Leopold Stokowski), Kurt Weill's United Nations anthem as part of his song cycle *Song of the Free*, and *They Are There!* by Charles Ives, often referred to as the father of American music, which expresses the notion of liberation and freedom through a blend of classical and avant-garde styles.
4. **Gebrauchsmusik**, or 'music for use': As defined by Paul Hindemith, Ernst Krenek, and Kurt Weill, this category refers to music created for specific purposes. German–American composer Kurt Weill sought to liberate opera from the confines of tradition. By incorporating new popular idioms like jazz and contemporary themes—such as *The Lindbergh Flight* (1929) and the sharp critique of urban life in *Rise and Fall of the City of Mahagonny* (1930)—Weill aimed to breathe new life into the musical theater of the Weimar Republic. During World War II, he contributed arrangements of patriotic songs like 'Battle Hymn of the Republic', 'Beat! Beat! Drums!', and 'The Star-Spangled Banner' to the American war effort. In the popular music of World War I and II, 'music of use' refers to songs published as sheet music and performed by soldiers or civilians to celebrate liberation and the newfound sense of freedom. These compositions were created, written, published, and performed within specific sociocultural and political contexts, often with a built-in expiration date—a sort of 'best used before the end of liberation'.

By understanding these different facets of liberation music, we can better appreciate its profound impact on both individual and collective memory, and its ability to shape our perception of freedom across time and space.

Rotterdams Glorie, cover (1945)

In the upcoming sections, I aim to focus on the categories of liberation songs (1) and Gebrauchsmusik (4). This music, resonating with the themes of freedom, hope, and the promise of a better future, offers a fascinating case study. The cover of the song *Rotterdams Glorie* is a good case in point where the sheet song already predates the restoration of the town's iconic building of faith in the musical terms of a freedom march. Compositions such as these allow us to see beyond the simplistic narrative that attributes the rise of American popular culture in the Netherlands solely to cultural imperialism.

Rather, the sonic landscape of the summer of 1945 was imbued with a deep sense of gratitude and celebration toward British, American, and Canadian influences. Many songs of the era captured this sentiment explicitly in their titles, such as *Sing Your Song of Thanks (to the Tommies and their Tanks)* or *America, We Thank You*. These compositions highlight a more nuanced and heartfelt response to the liberation, reflecting the joy and relief of a people embracing a newfound freedom, rather than merely the dominance of a foreign culture. The cover design captures this sense of pride and gratefulness by showing a young Dutch girl as the focus of attention in the middle of the image, resolute and strong-willed, supported by emblems of British and American supporters. Here, thankfulness is framed within a sense of trust, support, and dedication towards a common democratic goal.

2
WE DID IT BEFORE: SOUNDING INTERCULTURAL ENCOUNTERS

The popular sheet music I refer to as the 'soundtrack of liberation' holds a powerful expressive potential. The cover art, lyrics, music, and public

Sing your Song of Thanks (to the Tommies and their Tanks), cover (1945)

performances come together to serve as a medium for Dutch citizens to express themselves and affirm their identities after the liberation. These audiovisual and textual creations are more than just entertainment; they are responses to the cultural encounters with the various cultures of the liberators. Through the production and performance of this sheet music, people could articulate and represent their visions of both the past and the future.

I use the term 'imaginary' in the sense defined by Winfried Fluck, who describes it as 'the unstructured and decontextualized stream of images, associations, sensations, and feelings that constantly feed our cognition and interpretation of the world without having a tangible form of their own'.[28] In this context, the concept of 'liberation' takes on a central role in the European imagination from 1945 to the present. Consider, for example, the Liberation Route Europe, a digital multimedia project launched in 2013. This initiative offers a fresh multinational perspective on World War II, emphasizing the shared experience of liberation and the newfound sense of freedom. It poses an important question: How can we build a common European identity by drawing on our collective (media) memory of World War II, particularly positive elements like freedom and liberation?[29]

But what does this mean for the memory of the soundtrack of liberation? Is there a shared recollection of these songs? If we focus on the period when the sense of liberation was most vividly expressed through lyrics, songs, and music, we can trace the culture of liberation at a critical moment—just before, during, and immediately after the liberation of the Netherlands. This short but intense phase offers a unique glimpse into how a special human sensitivity was captured and communicated through the popular music of the time.

Eindelijk…, cover (1945)

The performance culture of Dutch liberation songs was not centered around showcasing special skills, musical talents, physical appeal, or technological feats. Instead, it embodied the concept of

Gebrauchsmusik—'music for use'—created for a specific national audience during the brief period between the launch of Operation Market Garden in September 1944 and the official liberation of the Netherlands, culminating in Nazi Germany's capitulation in May 1945. At that time, popular sheet music had not yet been overshadowed by what would soon become the dominant cultural forces: American movies and the recording industry. Before Dutch audiences were swept up in the allure of American sights, sounds, and fantasies, and before they absorbed these new realities, popular sheet music served as a vital medium for celebrating and expressing feelings of joy, pride, and gratitude. Despite the harsh realities of destroyed cities, war casualties, torn families, and uncertainty about missing loved ones, the overwhelming emotion during this period was a euphoric sense of freedom. This short-lived moment of anticipation and subsequent liberation gave rise to what can only be described as the magical summer of 1945. But once this period ended, the relevance of most of these songs faded, and very few were recorded or preserved in the collective memory.

What can we say about the music that filled the streets, bars, and public spaces during this time? The blueprint for Dutch liberation songs lay in American sheet music publications from the 1910s, when the cultural phenomena of jazz and later swing swept across Europe. These publications themselves drew on the tradition of 19th-century popular music, particularly minstrel songs. To some extent, the Dutch soundtrack of liberation was influenced by the rich archive of World War I sheet music and the interwar years.

World War I-era sheet music from the United States combined musical notes with lyrics and vibrant cover designs, which acted as visual gateways into the songs. The themes of these songs can be categorized as follows:

1. Celebrating American liberty with patriotic symbols like the flag and the Statue of Liberty.
2. Promoting the value of democracy.
3. Emphasizing the need to fight for American core values.
4. Commemorating key battles at Verdun, Flanders, or Berlin.
5. Identifying and satirizing the enemy.
6. Idealizing the lives of soldiers.
7. Expressing longing for loved ones overseas.

By World War II, the media landscape had become more complex. Soldiers not only relied on sheet music but also listened to the radio, watched films, played records, and attended live performances. Despite these new media, sheet music continued to play a crucial role. The sheer volume of songs published in the United States during the war suggests that this traditional medium was still effective in rallying support, fostering camaraderie among soldiers, stirring patriotism, and ridiculing or stigmatizing the enemy. The themes from World War I persisted into the 1940s, as evidenced by sheet music covers with titles like *Remember Pearl Harbor*, *Old Glory*, *Star Spangled Rhythm*, *Marching and Singing*, *Der Fuehrer's Face*, *Ten Little Soldiers*, *We Did It Before*, and *Praise the Lord and Pass the Ammunition!*

The opportunities for American media to shape perceptions of war and victory in World War II were more diverse than in earlier conflicts. The United States produced more war-related songs than any other country involved in the conflict. Hugo Keesing, a scholar and collector of sheet music, identified nine categories to capture the breadth of this sonic diplomacy:

1. Isolationism/Neutrality and conscription.
2. Focus on December 7, 1941—the attack on Pearl Harbor.
3. Songs about Hitler, Mussolini, Hirohito, Tojo, the Japanese, and others.
4. Highlighting the U.S. Army, Navy, Marines, Women in Service, etc.
5. Specific engagements such as the battle for Iwo Jima.
6. Subsets addressing rationing and shortages, blackouts, buying bonds, etc.
7. Songs dealing with separation, loneliness, etc.
8. Songs sung by or requested by the troops, such as 'Lili Marlene'.
9. Songs about the war's end and postwar adjustment.

The Dutch liberation songs embraced U.S. marketing strategies through elaborate cover art as a first means for potential buyers and performers to get an idea of what the song was about. The American patriotic song *We Did it Before and We Can Do it Again* by Cliff Friend and Charlie Tobias from 1941 is a good reference to how music has played an integral role in the history of war and the use of music. In a marching rhythm, the musicians and the listeners are persuaded to close ranks, join forces,

Covers of American WWII songs

and through the act of singing feel encouraged to fight for the cause of freedom. Before the song arrives at the snappy chorus, the verse ends with an assurance that through music the individual is connected with an army of millions in spirit and song: 'Millions of voices are ringing / Singing as we march along.' What had already proven to be an effective motivational media tool during the First World War found renewed success during the Second World War with the enduring message, 'We did it before, and we can do it again.' This refrain not only rallied troops and citizens alike but also established a cultural framework for hope and resilience that transcended national boundaries. The sentiment expressed in this phrase appears to resonate deeply with the themes of the Dutch liberation song *Eindelijk*—'Finally'. The cover art for *Eindelijk* vividly captures the spirit of this transformative moment. Central to the imagery is a celestial figure, an angel, triumphantly heralding a new dawn by blowing into a horn. This symbolic act represents the long-awaited arrival of freedom, signaling the end of oppression and the start of renewal.

The visual design of the cover further reinforces this theme of liberation through the inclusion of the American and British flags, which prominently frame the composition. These flags not only acknowledge the pivotal role of the Allied forces in the liberation of the Netherlands but also serve as cultural markers, suggesting the introduction of the liberators' rich cultural heritage into the postwar Dutch landscape. The angel, as a universal symbol of hope and divine intervention, bridges the emotional and spiritual dimensions of liberation with its physical and political realities. In this way, the song *Eindelijk* celebrates freedom and at the same reflects a collective aspiration for a brighter future, infused with the promise of intercultural exchange and unity.

We Did It Before, cover (1941)

What kind of music can we identify in the collection of Dutch liberation songs? Five categories are particularly relevant to expressing a new sense of freedom: hymns, love songs, marches, boogie-woogie and swing, and foxtrot songs. In the following section, I offer an overview of the various categories with references to the visual, textual, and sonic dimension of the compositions.

3
PEACE MARCH:
MARCHING MUSIC BETWEEN OCCUPATION AND FREEDOM

It may come as a surprise that marches—the very musical genre the National Socialists and the NSB (National Socialist Movement in the Netherlands) deemed most suitable for conveying authoritarian ideas and fascist esthetics—remained popular even after the war. Collections like *S.A. Liederbuch*, *Singendes Volk*, and *Kameradschaft im Lied*, along with nonfiction works such as Joseph Müller-Blattau's *Germanisches Erbe in Deutscher Tonkunst* (with a preface by Heinrich Himmler) and Richard Eichenauer's *Musik und Rasse*, show how the National Socialists recognized the power of marching music to de-individualize people, mold them into a controllable mass, and manipulate them into embracing a specific political ideology.[30] Youth groups often engaged in ritualistic singing and marches as a form of paramilitary exercise.

In the Netherlands, the popular collection of marches and war songs *Zoo zingt de NSB (Twintig Marsch- en Strijdliederen)* played a significant role in using music as a tool to 'educate' the young, transforming them into a uniform mass of soldiers. The motto 'Du bist nichts, dein Volk ist alles' (You are nothing, your people are everything) was effectively translated into the idea of marching in uniform rows, erasing any sense of individuality. Since May 1940, formations of the Nationale Jeugdstorm (National Youth Storm), Nederlandsche Arbeidsdienst (Dutch Labor Service), and the Dutch SS marched through the streets, singing songs like *Zwarthemdenlied*, *Vrijheid en Recht*, *WA Marcheert*, *Voorwaarts*, *Stormsoldaat*, and *Oostlandlied*[31]—the latter being sung by thousands of Dutch soldiers fighting on the Eastern Front.

Music and striking cover art combined to create an esthetic unity that found powerful expression in public marches and ritualistic festivals. Examples include the silhouetted rows of soldiers on the covers of *Singend door alle Dietsche gouwen* and *Lied der Legionssoldaten (Opgedragen aan wijlen zijne Luitenant Generaal H.A. Seyffardt)*. The fusion of marching music with political themes fostered a strong sense of unity among specific groups of people or soldiers. This type of music was designed to persuade, agitate, and overwhelm. When paired with uniforms, symbols, and color codes, the impact could be especially potent.[32] Certain expressions and musical motifs created easily recognizable reference points, with keywords like 'freedom', 'nation', 'flag', and 'fatherland' underscored by a marching beat and the fanfare-like rising fourth interval that typically marked the beginning of these songs.

But why would composers of liberation songs choose to draw on the same musical genre that had become synonymous with occupation, censorship, the loss of cultural identity, and national humiliation?

Judging by the cover art and lyrics, marching music became a powerful tool for reasserting freedom and reclaiming what had been lost. Songs like *We zijn weer Holland en we zijn weer vrij!*, *De Vrijheidsmars*, *Mijn Holland*,

Mijn Holland, cover (1945)

Vredesmarsch, and *Vry Nederland (Vryheidsmarsch)* illustrate how music can serve as a celebration of liberation from oppression. The symbols of the occupiers were now replaced by iconic images of windmills, Dutch flags, and the unchained Dutch lion.

The cover of *Bevrijdingslied* (Liberation Song) uses potent symbolism to communicate themes of triumph, resistance, and national pride. Central to the design is the Dutch lion, a national emblem, depicted in bold silhouette as it grasps a flagpole bearing the red, white, and blue Dutch tricolor. This imagery asserts the restoration of sovereignty and the resilience of the Dutch people. At the lion's feet lies a shattered swastika rendered in red and black, referring to the destruction of Nazi oppression and the liberation of the Netherlands. The minimalistic color palette, dominated by patriotic hues, emphasizes the significance of the flag and the broken swastika as visual focal points. Notably, the lyrics by A.B. Roosjen and music by Jo Juda were composed in the internment camp Kamp Sint-Michielsgestel, imbuing the piece with profound historical resonance. The cover encapsulates liberation as a reclamation of identity and defiance against tyranny.

Bevrijdingslied, cover (1945)

On May 5, 1945, the front page of *De Gelderlander* newspaper [then *Arnhems dagblad*] featured a poem beside an image of Queen Wilhelmina, where the metaphor of the Dutch lion served a similar purpose in both poetry and musical cover art.

De Hollandsche leeuw hoeft, Van woede verbeten, Niet langer onmachtig Gekerkerd te zijn.	The Dutch lion, Pent up with anger, Need no longer be impotent And encaged.

Rood Wit Blauw, cover (1945)

The color orange filled public spaces as a powerful symbol of regained freedom, serving as a visual counterpart to the resurgence of national identity through marching music. This color, deeply embedded in Dutch culture, even appeared in newspaper articles printed in orange after the liberation.[33] Alongside these visual cues, references to Dutch history, language, and the country's resilient spirit helped erase the five-year gap of humiliation and cultural colonization. Marching music with themes of freedom, nationhood, and patriotism allowed the Dutch people to confront and process the traumatic experiences of occupation and war.

The revival of Dutch marching music is closely linked to the emotions triggered by the sounds of 1940 to 1945. Consider the sonic landscape of occupation in the streets of major Dutch cities. In addition to the haunting wails of air raid sirens, the relentless drone of airplanes overhead, and the deafening explosions of bombs in city centers, Dutch war diaries often mention an eerie silence that followed the onset of occupation. In May 1940, traffic all but ceased—buses stopped running, taxis were unavailable, and due to fuel shortages, even doctors could only make house calls on bicycles. After October 1942, when all forms of musical performances were banned from the streets, Dutch citizens longed for the familiar tunes played by popular street organs. Church bells, too, fell silent as they were melted down for military use. Anne Frank poignantly described in her diary how she lost her sense of time when the Westerkerk bell stopped marking the hours for Amsterdam's citizens. The silencing of bells was accompanied by the loss of carillon music, while the sound of German troops singing their marching songs filled the void. In Amsterdam alone, 14,000 German soldiers contributed to the city's soundscape with their language and music. Many described the singing of German soldiers and NSB members as painfully off-key. Studies of Dutch war diaries reveal

Vry Nederland, cover (1945)

that one psychological strategy occupied citizens used to cope with the oppressive foreign cultural influence was to either ignore these sounds or categorize them as unpleasant.[34]

In 1944, a liberation song by Ar Colijn with a lively rhythm and catchy lyrics explicitly addressed the new sonic experience of hearing the bells ring again, as its title, *The Bells Now Ring Again*, suggests. The chorus captures this renewed sense of normalcy and hope:

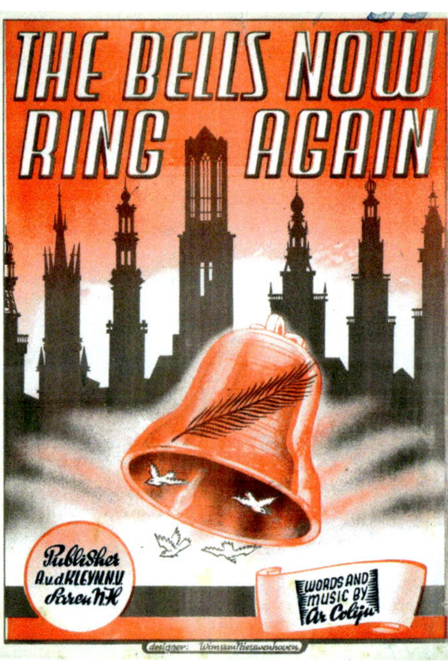

The Bells Now Ring Again, cover (1945)

The bells now ring again.
We did not wait in vain,
The sun drove out the rain
The Nazis slain,
Let's elevate our voice,
Sing to the Tommy boys
Our songs of gratitude.
In cheery mood.
All nightmares are ended,
Suddenly just as the war intended:
Liberty!!!
Now shake hands,
With Americans,
In steady brotherhood,
And cheery mood.

Envision the unique soundscape of 1945: the resurgence of bells ringing through devastated city centers, interwoven with marches like *Wij zijn weer vrij! (Lied van Vrijheid en Vrede)* with the Dutch lion on the cover proudly displaying weapons of war. Featuring lyrics by A.J. Driest and music by Hendrik van Beek, this piece was presented in a *gematigd Marschtempo met spontane voordracht*—a moderate marching tempo with spontaneous singing.

Uit de Cantine, cover (1945)

Wij zijn weer vrij!
Heft aan onz' jubel zangen.
Nu wij, verlost van slavernij,
Den vrede weer ontvangen.
Zoo moge dan die vrede
Ons hoeden voor hernieuwd geweld.
De vredes zonne stralen beschijnen
't eeuwig vredesveld.

We are free again!
Let us sing our jubilant songs.
Now that we, free from slavery,
Receive peace again.
So may that peace
Protect us from renewed violence.
The sunlight of peace shines
On the eternal field of peace.

The composer, Hendrik van Beek, notes that the final line of the chorus should be sung with great emphasis on melody and rhythm:

Zoo rijz' ons aller bede,
Dat voortaan t'allen tij
Op aarde heersche vreede
En Neerland blijve vrij!

Thus rise all of our prayers,
That from now on for all time
On earth shall reign peace
And the Netherlands be free!

The march concludes with a final fanfare on the rising C major chord, ending in a fortissimo that celebrates music, freedom, and peace. Keywords like 'rise', 'prayers', 'peace', and 'free' appear not only in this march but also in many other compositions that can be categorized as freedom marches.

We zijn weer Holland en we zijn weer vrij!, cover (1945)

4
HOLLAND MEMORIES: HYMNS TO FREEDOM AND JUSTICE

V-E Day, cover (1945)

A central theme in the genre of liberation songs is gratitude—gratitude for freedom regained, for the gift of life, and for the chance to embark on a new future. The *Gelderlander* headline on May 5, 1945 captures this sentiment in religious terms: 'God zij dank!' (Thank God!), followed by the line, 'Thank God it is over'. The front page features a well-known poem that connects the Dutch lion, a symbol of strength and power, with a spiritual advent, reflecting the long-awaited day of deliverance that finally came in May 1945. The keywords throughout resonate with liberty, gratitude, peace, and the promise of a new future.

En na het dankgebed	And after the prayer of thanks
Dat ons naar de lippen welt,	Which wells up to our lips
Mag de jubel losbreken	Jubilation may burst forth
Over onze straten en huizen.	In our streets and homes.

The musical genre that many composers employed to provide a musical underscore for these emotions consisted of secular music and religious hymns. Several songs like *Het Vrij Nederland*, *Vrede*, *Holland, een Hymne*, and others build on traditional religious tunes to commemorate the new sense of freedom and to give praise to God for having liberated the Dutch people from evil:

Hallelujah! 't loflied prijze Hem,	Hallelujah! Praise to Him,
Die onze banden slaakt!	Who breaks our chains!
Hij zal Israël doen verrijzen!	He will give rise to Israel!
Maar ook Holland vrij Hij maakt!	But He also makes Holland free!

Hij zal Israël doen verrijzen!
Maar ook Holland vrij Hij maakt!

He will give rise to Israel!
But He also makes Holland free!

Vrij is Nederland, cover (1945)

These hymns were sung together in churches. Thus, through collective singing, communities actively reinforced social cohesion. Accompanied by the organ, often referred to as the 'queen of instruments', hymns express the healing power of music to overcome moments of crisis, be it spiritual or national.[35] Singing hymns provides a crucial part of what Benedict Anderson described as an 'imagined community'. His constructive approach suggests that the category 'nation' needs to be separated from objective values and rather be considered as a flexible product of the shared thinking, practices, and communication of a group of people. The imagination of a community allows its members to engage in the fantasy of sharing beliefs, values, traditions, and memories, although the members might never meet or know each other. However, 'in the minds of each lives the image of their communion'.[36] Other songs, like Tom Erich's hymn *Vrijheid en Recht* based on a text by Anton Beuving, combine hymnic structures with national pathos. The chorus emphasizes a new world order after times of war:

Vrijheid en Recht, cover (1945)

Vrijheid en recht,	Freedom and Justice,
Nooit meer geknecht,	Nevermore suppressed,
Geen vrees meer voor barbaren	No more fear of barbarians
Wij bouwen en wij varen!	We build and we sail!
Vrijheid en recht,	Freedom and Justice,
De grondsteen gelegd	The keystone is placed
Voor vrede en gerechtigheid	For peace and justice
Na vijf jaaren van strijd!	After five years of fighting.

The fusion of political events like the liberation with religious expressions of gratitude in the ritualistic act of singing during services helped to forge a strong bond among those who had been humiliated during the Nazi occupation. Walker Connor captures the essence of the imagined community concept by stating, '(...) what ultimately matters is not what is, but what people believe is'.[37] Framing the liberation of the Netherlands in religious terms offered singers and participants in church rituals the opportunity to embrace a spiritual framework that restored their dignity, identity, and sense of national belonging.

Holland Memories, cover (1945)

5
LILI MARLEEN:
TRANSATLANTIC AND TRANSNATIONAL WAR SONGS

Love songs have always held a significant place in human history. However, during times of crisis like World War II, they take on a particularly vital, compensatory, and sometimes controversial role. These songs offer an outlet for expressing grief, sorrow, and longing for loved ones, whether lost to death or whose fate remains uncertain. For example, after various defeats, BBC radio programmers strategically used music to boost the morale of workers in factories and soldiers on the front lines. They banned sentimental songs and crooners, believing that such music could weaken the resolve of troops abroad and challenge traditional notions of masculinity during wartime.[38]

Vrijheid en Recht, cover (1945)

In the liberation song collection, compositions like *Ver en Toch Nabij!* (*Just a Prayer Away*) and *Wees Maar Gerust* are prime examples of this genre. The latter was originally composed by the German musician Gerhard Winkler and published under the title *Mach dir um mich bitte keine Sorgen*. In the Netherlands, singer Nelly Verschuur popularized the song with Dick Willebrandts and his dance orchestra, featuring new lyrics by Han Dunk. Written in 1943 from the perspective of a soldier in the field, the song tells of tender letters of love from his homeland. The lovers express their feelings for each other, with the soldier reassuring his beloved that he will remain faithful to their shared future. While the Dutch lyrics mostly adhere to the German original, they also contain a hidden code. In the chorus, where the German version says, 'My heart tells me that you will come back home for sure' ('Mir sagt mein Herz, du kommst bestimmt nach Haus'), the Dutch translation subtly subverts the seemingly innocent

APOLLO
No 435
Lili Marleen
NACH GEDICHTEN
VON
HANS LEIP
MUSIK:
NORBERT SCHULTZE
APOLLO-VERLAG PAUL LINCKE
BERLIN SW 68
für Gesang
und Klavier

Lili Marlen
Lire 4.-
MUSICA DI
NORBERT SCHULTZE
EDIZIONI SUVINI ZERBONI
MILANO

Lilli Marlene
My Lilli Of The Lamplight
BY NORBERT SCHULTZE, HANS LEIP,
AND TOMMIE CONNOR
Featured by
MARY SMALL
PUBLISHED & DISTRIBUTED IN THE PUBLIC INTEREST
WITH THE CONSENT OF THE ALIEN PROPERTY CUSTODIAN
UNDER LICENSE NO. E565
MADE IN U.S.A.
Edward B. Marks Music Corporation RCA Bldg., Radio City, New York

THE SONG HIT OF THE ALLIED FORCES!
Lilli Marlene
PRICE
40¢
Featured by
DON TURNER
and his orchestra
Published in Canada by
Gordon V. Thompson Limited

THE ONLY AUTHENTIC PETER MAURICE VERSION
OF THE FAMOUS INTERNATIONAL HIT
Lilli Marlene
My Lilli Of The Lamplight
BY NORBERT SCHULTZE, HANS LEIP,
AND TOMMIE CONNOR
All performing credits must be given to
Peter Maurice Music Co., Ltd.
(Member British Performing Right Society)
Sung Exquisitely
by
JOAN BROOKS
MADE IN U.S.A.
Edward B. Marks Music Corporation RCA Bldg., Radio City, New York

THE ONLY AUTHENTIC PETER MAURICE VERSION
OF THE FAMOUS INTERNATIONAL HIT
Lilli Marlene
My Lilli Of The Lamplight
BY NORBERT SCHULTZE, HANS LEIP,
AND TOMMIE CONNOR
All performing credits must be given to
Peter Maurice Music Co., Ltd.
(Member British Performing Right Society)
PRICE 60c
Sung Exquisitely
by
ANNE SHELTON
ON LONDON RECORD NO. 144
PUBLISHED & DISTRIBUTED IN THE PUBLIC INTEREST
WITH THE CONSENT OF THE ALIEN PROPERTY CUSTODIAN
UNDER LICENSE NO. E565
MADE IN U.S.A.
EDWARD B. MARKS MUSIC CORPORATION · 136 WEST 52nd STREET · NEW YORK 19, N.Y.

love song with the line 'Wees maar gerust, 't gaat alles weer voorbij'. This phrase, 'Rest assured, one day it will all be over', could refer not only to the soldier's dangerous situation but also to the harsh reality of the German occupation, making the song a coded message of hope for the end of the war in the minds of Dutch listeners.

In Great Britain, the BBC employed a similar technique by turning to German classical music. For instance, the famous leitmotif at the beginning of Ludwig van Beethoven's Fifth Symphony was used as the opening for their broadcast *Der Deutsche Dienst* to inform German soldiers and citizens of the dire situation on the frontlines after 1941, countering the propaganda of Joseph Goebbels. Émigré artist Carl Brinitzer incorporated the Beethoven motif at the start of the news reports, played by timpani as a sort of musical alert. When translated into Morse code, the rhythmic structure of the motif (three shorts, one long) corresponds to the letter 'V'—signifying 'victory'.[39]

Other songs, like *Tulips Bloom in Holland Once Again*, paid tribute to the stereotypes of Dutch culture familiar to Americans through earlier hits like Bing Crosby's *Little Dutch Mill*, which topped the charts in 1934, and Glenn Miller's popular 1940 tune *In an Old Dutch Garden (By an Old Dutch Mill)*. The song *Snoezepoes* even quotes the Miller hit almost verbatim in its first line: 'By the old Dutch mill we were sitting hand in hand.'

One song, however, stands out: *Onder de Lantaren*, the Dutch version of *Lili Marleen*, arguably the most popular song of World War II. While some label it a Nazi song, others describe it as a transnational hymn of love and peace. But how can a song be both a tool of Hitler's war propaganda and an anthem of liberation? The original lyrics by Hans Leip (1893–1983) and the music by Norbert Schultze (1911–2002) underwent a remarkable transformation as they crossed national boundaries, re-emerging in different languages, new arrangements, and various interpretations by different artists.

In our collective memory, *Lili Marleen* is so closely associated with the sights and sounds of World War II that it's difficult to imagine its origins in the experience of World War I. The writer and poet Hans Leip from Hamburg explained that on the night of April 3, 1915, at the barracks in Berlin, he jotted down the lines about two women he was in love with: one called Lili, the other Marlene. Fearing that any day he might be sent to the front and never return to his love, he began composing both the verses and a melody while gazing at a lamppost nearby. The identities of the two women merged into the name *Lili Marleen*. Singing and humming to himself helped Leip cope with the anguish of war.

When Leip published the lyrics in 1937 in a booklet titled *Die kleine Hafenorgel* (*The Little Harbor Song Collection*), he added two additional verses that introduced a surprisingly morbid tone. What begins as a naïve love song ends with the whispered longing of a dead soldier emerging from his grave. No other song of the twentieth century has been translated into as many different languages—scholars have counted 48 so far. However, the romanticization of death and the ghostly atmosphere are unique to the German version, particularly in the fifth and final verse:

Aus dem stillen Raume,	Out of the silent emptiness,
Aus der Erde Grund	Out of earth's ground
Hebt mich wie im Träume	Lifts me, as if in a dream,
Dein verliebter Mund	Your loving mouth
Wenn sich die späten Nebel drehn	When the fogs at twilight turn
Werd' ich bei der Laterne steh'n	I will stand at the lantern.
|: Wie einst Lili Marleen. :|	|: Like once Lili Marlene. :|

The fourth (and final) verse of the Dutch version *Onder de Lantaren* by Herre de Vos picks up on the sentimentality of loss and melancholy. However, De Vos avoids the gloomy atmosphere of the German version in favor of a more romantic image such as sailing across the ocean facing the forces of nature:[40]

Onder de lantaren,	Underneath the lantern
Loop jij nu, mijn kind…	ou now walk, my child…
Ik ben weer gaan varen:	I have gone out sailing:
En zwalk door weer en wind.	And roam through rain and storm.
Soms is mijn hart zoo zwaar als steen	Sometimes my heart is heavy as a stone.
En dan gaan mijn gedachten heen	And then my thoughts go drifting home
|: Naar jou, Lili Marleen. :|	|: To you, Lili Marlene. :|

This page and p. 60:
Lili Marlene covers from Germany, Italy, Canada, America, America, America, France, Italy, and Great Britain

The song was published in several countries, including Italy, Germany, Canada, the United States, and Great Britain. It was so successful that in 1949, Tommie Connor and Johnny Reine composed a follow-up version called *The Wedding of Lili Marlene*. It appeared in the Netherlands under the title *De Trouwdag van Lili Marlene*, with Dutch lyrics by Bart Ekkers. Despite the continued popularity of these songs around the world, *Lili Marleen* did not initially start out as a hit. In 1939, Electrola Records planned to record *Lili Marleen* with Lale Anderson. They accepted a new musical arrangement by Norbert Schultze, who would later become infamous as 'Bomber Schultze' due to his notorious Nazi marching music. However, the record did not sell particularly well at first. It was only when Radio Belgrade in Yugoslavia, with its extensive broadcast range to German troops in the Balkans and Austria, included *Lili Marleen* in its *Wunschkonzert* series that the song became a favorite among German soldiers. *Lili Marleen* was broadcast every night at 10 o'clock, preceded by the military *Zapfenstreich* as a signal for the troops to retire. In this way, the unique combination of media, occupation, and military musical rituals added a new 'sonic layer' to *Lili Marleen*.

The tremendous international success of *Lili Marleen* is also tied to a legend in North Africa. When German soldiers listened to the song at night, British forces on the other side of the front were said to have shouted for them to turn up the volume of the radio. In *Escape to Adventure* (1950), the British diplomat and politician Fitzroy Maclean recalled the powerful emotions stirred by hearing Lale Anderson sing *Lili Marleen* in the spring of 1942: 'Husky, sensuous, nostalgic, sugar-sweet, her voice seemed to reach out to you, as she lingered over the catchy tune, the sickly sentimental words'.[41]

British officials later asked writer Tommie Connor to add new English lyrics in order to obscure the song's German origins. He provided the now-famous title *Lili of the Lamplight* and removed the final two verses, which referenced death and a ghostly doppelgänger. When *Time* magazine featured an article about the propaganda film *The True Story of Lili Marlene*, Marlene Dietrich decided to record a new version. In her rendition, the lantern in front of the barrack was replaced by a 'corner light'. Marlene Dietrich, like no other singer, played a pivotal role in 'de-Nazifying' the tune, transforming it into a universal song of love and longing that transcended time and place. At the Allied front, *Lili Marleen* gradually shed its military identity as a soldier's song, emerging from Marlene Dietrich's lips as a smooth, melancholy love song that transcended nations and politics.

Outside the barracks
By the corner light
I'll always stand and wait for you at night
We will create a world for two
I'll wait for you the whole night through
For you, Lili Marlene
For you, Lili Marlene

Bugler, tonight don't play the call to arms
I want another evening with its charms
Then we will say goodbye and pass
I'll always keep you in my heart
With me, Lili Marlene
With me, Lili Marlene

When we are marching in the mud and cold
And when my pack seems more than I can hold
My love for you renews my might
I'm warm again, my pack is light
It's you, Lili Marlene
It's you, Lili Marlene.[42]

The different orchestration of *Lili Marleen* created different contexts for the emotional fantasies. The military opening sounds changed from a soldier's horn to a melancholy accordion. Dietrich's intonation often exaggerates the sentimentality of love and longing. The rhythm includes swing elements. Instead of gothic gloom and the ghostly lover emerging from the grave at the end of the German version, Dietrich emphasizes renewed hope for a better future with the lover reunited with Lili Marlene.

The Wedding of Lilli Marlene, cover (1949)

In 1942, the song *De soldaat en het meisje / Der Soldat und das Mädchen* capitalized on the success of *Lili Marleen*. The lyrics in Dutch by Jean Bouvet and in German by Bernd Rüsing celebrated the life of a soldier (albeit in the occupied Netherlands). The cover tells of the proud soldiers parading through public spaces drawing the attention of young women. While the Dutch lyrics simply refer to soldiers going out to have a good time with the girls, the German version refers to the typical scene of meeting Lili Marlene 'outside the big gate' of the military camp. 'When our daily shift is over, many a young girl waits outside the gate, free and clear, for her soldier.'

After 1945, the German émigré and naturalized American citizen Marlene Dietrich presented *Lili Marleen* as the signature tune of her concert tours, often introducing it in the following way: 'Now, here is a song that is very close to my heart. I sang it during the war. I sang it for three long years, all through Africa, Sicily, Italy, to Alaska, Greenland, Iceland, to England, through France, through Belgium, [with a long pause] to Germany, and to Czechoslovakia. The soldiers loved it, *Lili Marleen*.' She might have also mentioned that she sang the song in the Netherlands, perhaps during her performances in Maastricht, which brought her in contact not only with American troops but also with the Dutch population.[43] With its German origins, European interpretations and American mediations, the song became a transnational denominator in WWII with its theme of 'love conquers all'.

Der Soldat und das Meisje, cover (1942)

While women played an important role as love interests during and after the war, it is noteworthy that in the American musical context, the war effort and liberation was also tied to the role played by women active in the military service.[44] Before 'Rosie' had been established as a common signifier for women in the military workforce, she was known to the American radio audience under different names such as 'Anna with a Red Bandana',

'The Damsel from Douglas', 'Minnie (Who Is in It for the Money)', 'Plain Jane Doe', and 'Pluggin' Jane'. Most of the male lyricists used the literary device of combining a popular female name with a reference to a workspace beyond the domestic sphere to generate a sense of curiosity. At least 25 popular songs became the basis for a remarkable process of remediation: *Anna She Wears a Red Bandanna, Convairina, Damsel from Douglas, The Dig Down Sister (Dig Down on the Farm), Fighting on the Home Front, WINS, From the Old Swing Shift to the Kitchen, Helping Her Honey Hurry Home, How Will We Get Her Back in the Kitchen (After We've Won the War), The Lady's on the Job, Let's Keep the Corsairs Flying High, Mama, Put Your Britches On, Minnie's in the Money, Miss Victory, Mom's Building Bombers Now, My Gal's Working at Lockheed, My Girls is a Regular Girl, My Little W.O.W., Plain Jane Doe, Pluggin' Jane, Rosie the Riveter, She's that Airplane Working Baby of Mine, Sweetheart in Overalls, A Worker in a War Plant, The W.O.W. Song, You Look Good in Them Pants*.

Among these propaganda tunes, the song *Rosie the Riveter* with words and music by Redd Evans and John Jacob Loeb was particularly successful. Although the title of the song adheres to the scheme of many other products of the same type and features a groovy boogie-woogie rhythm with close harmonies, one thing stands out musically. The composers include a sonic gimmick: a verbal imitation of a riveting gun. The crooner is asked to insert the special sound between the words 'Rosie' and 'the riveter' creating a sense of joyful anticipation. The music is supposed to fall silent with a 'tacet' while the composers ask the singer to 'imitate the sound of a riveting machine: "brrrrrr".'[45] The musical break with its sonic effect is striking, humorous and highly recognizable. This musical sound effect might be one of the reasons why we identify American women in the military workforce as Rosies rather than Annas, Minnies, or Janes.

Visually, the cover art of the sheet song is in line with similar compositions showing attractive young women in unusual gender roles. For example, *You Look Good in Them Pants* with words and music by Abe Samya and Charles Wagner features two drawings of a blond and dark-haired girl who are depicted in a barn with a pitchfork and with a hammer on a work bench. Special emphasis is put on the women wearing red and blue pants to prove that visual attraction is not limited to traditional female costumes. The lyrics also comment on women's appeal while doing patriotic work.

'But when you see them in the shop they spin around like a top/ Making guns and planes they really did their job./ And over on the farm, working happy and gay/ Raising the crops our nation needs ev'ry day' (transcription by Keesing). The song leaves no doubt, however, that the exchange of jobs and clothes was only a temporary affair before women would be expected to return to prewar gender codes: 'But, darling, I wonder now that the war is over/ Will you and your ma take off them pants./ I'll shout and say ev'ry dog has his day/ Take off them pants so we will have a chance' (transcription by Keesing). The hope for a conservative backlash after the war was over, as can be gleaned from the title of another song which frames the return to traditional gender roles as a question: *How Will We Get Her Back in the Kitchen (After We've Won the War)?*[46] Surprisingly, the song by Billy Hayes, Zeb Carver, and Jack Rollin ends with a reference to a change of gender roles that might be irreversible—at least for the time being. 'She thinks it's patriotic so there is nothing I can say./ The hand that rocked the cradle is the hand that rules today.'[47]

The cover of *Pluggin' Jane* by Perry Alexander offers an elaborate collage of a young dark-haired woman smiling at the viewer with bright red lips and a blue shirt. Behind her stands Uncle Sam in patriotic drag proudly presenting the young female worker who is making sure that all the other women in the military receive their orders. Eleven additional figures on the cover's lower half and on the right side show women working in factories, as messengers, pilots, or in military intelligence. On the far right we also catch a glimpse of a girl with a red bandana. The lyrics emphasize that Jane is a kind of free-floating signifier for women doing their share in the war effort: 'Oh! Pluggin' Jane keeps pluggin ev'ry day/ She has no time to play, just plugs along all day/ Pluggin' Jane, she's pluggin' all the time/ And doing mighty fine on our assembly line./ She drives a rivet in our mighty ship/ So we can give it to the Jerry and the Nip.'[48] The cover that comes closest to the one on *Rosie the Riveter* is the one for *The Damsel from Douglas*. The song ironically makes a case that the object of the male love interest, a female riveter working for Douglas Aircraft Company, is more attractive than the Rosie who allegedly works for the American aerospace company Lockheed Corporation. The cover in shades of red features a slender woman concentrating on her work on the riveting gun with a visual reference to an American bomber shooting down an enemy aircraft.

Sheet music covers for American songs about women in the war industry: *You Look Good in Them Pants, Pluggin' Jane, The Damsel from Douglas,* and *Rosie the Riveter*

Next to her is the male protagonist of the song who is awaiting training on how to rivet. The lyrics not only create a competition about which girl is the prettier one but also who is writing the best propaganda song about women at war. 'You've heard about Rosie the Riveter/ The lady from Lockheed is nice/ But I've got a song that will ring the gong/ And put all of the others on ice.'[49]

The cover of the most successful and influential song, *Rosie the Riveter*, zooms in on one of the workers on a riveting machine. The slender girl with striking red hair and red lips not only helps to produce bomber planes for the military, in this case the song talks about a Douglas XB-19, the largest U.S. bomber aircraft at the time. She also produces sounds that come across as musical notes emanating from the riveting gun. Thus, the cover emphasizes the very musical gimmick that helped to make the song highly recognizable and different from other tunes with a similar theme.

Rosie the Riveter became a smash hit in 1942. The U.S. War Information campaign produced posters, cover art, photo series, and films that assigned political roles to American women, who increasingly came to be identified with the name 'Rosie'. First, these women were seen as a new force in the military war machine, one that would reach the shores of Europe through the weapons they produced. Second, the multimedia propaganda efforts had far-reaching effects, both nationally and internationally. Third, the line about sabotage in the song's lyrics suggests that women had become integral to a surveillance system aimed at identifying, denouncing, and eliminating potentially subversive forces within the U.S. population and workforce: 'Keeps a sharp lookout for sabotage / Sitting up there on the fuselage, / That little frail can do / More than a male can do, / Rosie (brrrrrr) the riveter.' Popular music, coupled with the intermedial nature of sheet music, served as a powerful tool for reaching a large audience. The song's reference to an all-American girl named 'Rosie' provided the template for Norman Rockwell's *Saturday Evening Post* cover featuring 'Rosie the Riveter' on May 29, 1943, six months after the song gained popularity. On the cover, a muscular young woman sits confidently in front of the American flag, holding a large riveting gun in her right hand, a sandwich in her left, with her foot resting firmly on Hitler's *Mein Kampf*.

In contrast, the Dutch liberation genre emphasized the beauty of women while leaving the active role in intercultural encounters to men. This shift towards more traditional gender roles is evident in the titles of the songs, where women are portrayed more as love interests than as independent, powerful, and accomplished members of the workforce. Despite this, the musical soundtrack remained similar, as we will explore in the following chapter. The twenty-five titles were selected from a sample of more than 300 published sheets depicting women in non-military roles.[50]

6
WHITE STRIPES IN A SKY OF BLUE: FOX-TROTTING AND FLIRTING

One of the most popular themes in liberation songs was the foxtrot dance, which is understandable given its origins. The foxtrot emerged in the United States during the 1910s, resulting from the collaboration between innovative British dancers Vernon and Irene Castle and the influential African American musician James Reese Europe. Allegedly, Jim Europe and Ford Dabney of Harlem's Clef Club wrote so many songs and marches that their names were sometimes spelled backwards on sheet music to 'lend an appearance of variety'.[51] After the dance craze swept across the United States in the early 20th century, the foxtrot quickly became a transatlantic sensation by the 1930s. American artists traveled throughout Europe, and foxtrot music became the singing and dancing phenomenon of the interwar years, sold through records, sheet music, and broadcast on radios. European composers embraced the format, creating songs for their respective national audiences. By the 1940s, Dutch composers drew on this rich history and experience with foxtrot music to express humor and joy at the newfound freedom.

Liefde in Rhythme, cover (1945)

Many of these songs capture the exhilarating atmosphere of intercultural encounters between Dutch citizens and Allied forces from Canada, the UK, and the United States. In a lighthearted manner, they often poke fun at cultural misunderstandings or language barriers. Examples include Jack Millar's *White Stripes in a Sky of Blue*, dedicated to the Allied Air Forces 'who in the cause of freedom, flew over Holland'. Jack Bulterman frequently used situational comedy in his lyrics to highlight the playful nature of cross-cultural interactions. In his foxtrot

Snoezepoes, an Allied soldier encounters every conceivable stereotype of a romantic rendezvous with a Dutch girl: sitting 'by the old Dutch mill', holding hands, whispering words of love under a linden tree, and wearing wooden shoes. Alas, neither understood a word the other said. The only Dutch word the soldier learns and lovingly remembers is the term for 'sweetheart'—*snoezepoes*. Similarly, Bulterman uses lively songs to create linguistic bridges. In *Da-ag, Da-ag, Da-ag!*, Allied soldiers receive a playful lesson in how to win the hearts of the Dutch.

Tommies, Canadians, Boys from the U.S.A.—
If you meet someone and want to greet someone,
Here's the word you've got to say:
Da-ag, Da-ag, Da-ag!
How I like this way to say: 'Hello!'
Da-ag, Da-ag, Da-ag!
It's the only word of Dutch I know
But it's enough to tell you
That I am glad to see you!

Jack Bulterman, a composer as well as multitalented musician on piano, trumpet, and accordion, is a key figure in the liberation song genre. He built on his work for The Ramblers and translated cabaret elements to the experience of liberation between 1944 and 1945. His light and joyful songs must have struck a chord with both the Dutch citizens and the liberators.[52]

Many liberation songs express gratitude towards the liberators in songs like *Thanks Tommies!* or *Sing your Song of Thanks (to the Tommies and their Tanks)*. Some of the most memorable songs address romantic encounters using a humorous mix of Dutch and English lyrics in songs like *Geef mij maar 'n echt Hollandsch Meisje* (I prefer a real Dutch Girl), *Little Holland Girl, Mamma, zijn naam is Johnny*, or *Mijn Tommy uit Canada*. Among the liberation songs *Trees heeft een Canadees* is one of the few to have left a lasting imprint on Dutch cultural memory

Trees heeft een Canadees	Trees has got a Canadian
O, wat is dat kindje in haar sas	Oh, how smitten the child is
Trees heeft een Canadees	Trees has got a Canadian

Samen in de 'jeep' en dan: vol gas!	Together in the jeep and then full throttle
Al vindt zij dat Engels lang niet mis is,	Though she thinks English isn't half bad,
Wil zij dolgraag weten wat een kiss is	She really wants to know what a 'kiss' is
Trees heeft een Canadees	Trees has got a Canadian
O, wat is dat kindje in haar sas.	Oh, how smitten the child is.

The jeep was just one of many items that showcased the bond between liberators and Dutch girls in public. One of the most iconic and enduring images etched into the collective cultural memory features Allied soldiers riding through Dutch towns on motorcycles, often with jubilant young Dutch women seated on the back. These scenes, captured in photographs and postcards, serve as precious reminders of the joy, relief, and optimism that permeated the summer of 1945, as the Dutch looked forward to a new era of freedom and peace after years of occupation. One particularly memorable photograph, showing a Canadian liberator on a motorcycle with two Dutch girls, has been immortalized in numerous postcards, sym-

Amstellaan (Vrijheidslaan)—May 8, 1945, Canadian liberator on a motorbike with two Dutch girls. Freedom Museum Archive

Postcard showing an Allied soldier on a motorbike with two Dutch women

bolizing the deep gratitude and camaraderie shared between the Dutch and their Allied liberators.

The postcards embellish the images with tulips and flags, highlighting the renewed national spirit of happiness, joy, and pride. In one postcard, by T.L. Lensen, British and Dutch flags are adorned with colorful ribbons on both the motorbike and in the streets. The Dutch text on the postcard, translated into English, reads: 'They asked him where he came from. He answered, Jan Steenstraat, Amsterdam.'[53]

Another postcard, likely designed for soldiers to send home, includes references to the love affair between a British liberator and a Dutch girl, written in three languages: French, Dutch, and English. The English version, though, contains a small spelling mistake, suggesting it was hastily created to capture the spirit of the moment. The scene depicted is titled 'The Tommie and his Guide', with the guide being a Dutch girl, presumably knowledgeable about where the next party or dance is happening.

We know these scenes were widespread not only due to the numerous references found across various media—such as photographs, postcards,

Postcard showing an Allied soldier on a motorbike with a Belgian woman

and songs—but also through personal artifacts like the inscription on the back of a photograph. The image, depicting an Allied liberator with two young girls, bears the handwritten note: 'Bevrijding – natuurlijk even met de eerste Canadees op de motor' ('Liberation—Of course, briefly with the first Canadian on a motorcycle'). This casual mention of 'of course' reflects just how familiar and commonplace it was for young Dutch girls to be photographed with the liberating soldiers, particularly Canadians.[54]

As curator Rense Havinga highlights, the use of 'of course' in this context speaks volumes about the shared experience of liberation. It suggests that posing with the first arriving Canadian soldiers, often seen on motorcycles, became an almost symbolic gesture of celebration. The act was so ingrained in the social fabric of the time that it felt like a natural, expected moment for those experiencing the joy of liberation firsthand. These small yet significant interactions between liberators and civilians were not only a mark of gratitude and excitement but also part of the collective memory of a nation emerging from occupation.[55]

While *Trees heeft een Canadees* is comparatively well-known, recorded and performed regularly, the story it tells is by no means an exception in the liberation song genre. Songs like *Snoezepoes*, *Da–ag, Da–ag, Da–ag,* (followed by the self-ironic line 'It's the only word of Dutch I know' in the catchy chorus) or *Weet je Wat een Zoentje is? Een Zoentje is 'A Little Kiss',* deal with similar issues using mixed language lyrics as a means to humorously address intercultural encounters between Allied soldiers and Dutch girls:

Weet je wat een zoentje is?	Do you know what a kiss is?
Een zoentje is 'a little kiss',	A kiss is 'a little kiss',
Een meisje is 'a little miss'.	A girl is 'a little miss'.
That's all, my darling!	That's all, my darling!
Hoe gaat het heet	How do you do
'How do you do?'	'How do you do?'
Ik hou van jou is	I love you is
'I love you.'	'I love you.'
Dat is de waarheid,	That is the truth,
'That is true.'	'That is true.'
That's all, my darling!	That's all, my darling!

Weet je Wat een Zoentje is?, cover (1945)

Music, flirting with Allied soldiers, and American entertainment culture became integral parts of social life in 1945. The popularity of the foxtrot was bolstered by novel dances like the Lindy Hop and the Jitterbug.[56] Several Dutch sheet music pieces from 1945 included more or less detailed instructions for the dance moves meant to accompany the music. Examples include *De Hi Ha Holland Dans* and the so-called dance sensation from Great Britain, *The Chestnut Tree*. One of the most memorable and impactful dances from this period is *De Sten-Gun*

White Stripes in a Sky of Blue, cover (1945)

Walk—a musical tribute to resistance fighter Pierre Zom, Jr. After the war, a pianist discovered a large cache of British Sten guns hidden beneath the dance floor of Zom's dance school. In recognition of Zom's courageous role during the occupation, Leo Friedriks (aka Fred Riks) composed a song about Sten guns and developed an elaborate choreography, allowing dancers to joyfully reenact the liberation of the Dutch people. In this way, music and performance created a unifying experience of self-empowerment, capturing the unique spirit of freedom felt in 1945.

Holland vrij! Ieder blij.	Holland free! Everybody happy.
En een het Nederlandsche Volk	And all of the Dutch people
Dans nu de 'Sten-Gun Walk'.	Now dance the 'Sten Gun Walk'.
Hold your Sten!	Hold your Sten!
Pas op je tellen!	Watch your step!
Hold your Sten!	Hold your Sten!
Tred niet versnellen!	Don't walk too fast!

Many love songs from this period explore the new and exhilarating relationships with Canadian soldiers, who, unlike the British or American liberators, stayed longer in the Netherlands to secure the territory. As Rense Havinga points out, these romantic entanglements were viewed with a degree of suspicion by the older generation. 'The gratitude expressed towards the Allied soldiers was enormous, with girls fighting over who could kiss a soldier first, and parents turning a blind eye to many of these intimate encounters. The liberators, after all, deserved some reward for their efforts. Hadn't attention from women always been the reward for military heroes? In the imagery of the time, the Netherlands itself was often represented as a woman, embracing her male liberators. Within this context, a Dutch girl dancing with an Allied soldier was seen as fulfilling her duty on behalf of a grateful nation.'[57]

In this unique climate of intercultural encounters, composers produced a substantial number of love songs to commemorate these moments. Typical titles include *Mijn Tommy uit Canada* and *Mamma, zijn naam is Johnny*. The arrival of the Canadian army was heralded as a sign of joy and hope for better times. The song *Daar komen de Canadezen*, from May 1945, expresses this admiration for soldiers who came from afar with the mission to liberate the Netherlands:

Here come the Canadians,
They came from across the ocean,
They risked their blood and their lives,
They stood in storms of bullets,

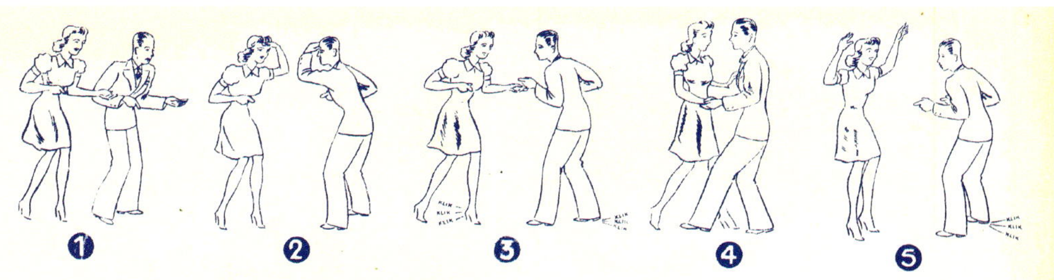

Dansinstituut Pierre Zom Jr. - 's-Gravendijkwal 130

„MEMBER OF THE IMPERIAL SOCIETY OF TEACHERS OF DANCING"

PRESENTEERT DE NIEUWE GEZELSCHAPSDANS VAN 1945

DE „STEN-GUN WALK"

DANSBESCHRIJVING:

FIG. 1 — 3 MATEN

L. vt. voorwaarts (Trucking-walk) . . . . . Q Q
R. vt. voorwaarts „ „ . . . . . Q Q
L. vt. voorwaarts „ „ . . . . . Q Q
R. vt. voorwaarts „ „ . . . . . Q Q
op deze pas gelijk een kwart draai rechtsom maken dame links om zoodat dame en heer nu met de gezichten naar elkaar toestaan
L. vt. zijwaarts . . . . Slow
R. vt. herplaatsen . . . . Slow
3 maten

FIG. 2 — 1 MAAT

Dame en heer met linker hand boven de oogen.
Heer naar rechts, dame naar links kijken . . Slow
Heer naar links, dame naar rechts kijken . . Slow
1 maat

FIG. 1 — 2 MATEN

L. vt. voorwaarts (Trucking-walk) . . . . . Q Q
R. vt. voorwaarts „ „ . . . . . Q Q
op deze pas een kwartdraai rechtsom maken (dame weer linksom op L. vt.)
L. vt. zijwaarts . . . . Slow
R. vt. het gewicht er op terug laten komen . Slow
2 maten

FIG. 2 — 1 MAAT

Met linkerhand horizontaal boven de oogen naar rechts kijken dame naar links . . . . Slow
Met linkerhand horizontaal boven de oogen naar elkaar kijken . . . . Slow
1 maat

FIG. 3 — 1 MAAT

De beweging maken als heeft men een sten-gun in aanslag met de rechter wijsvinger heen en weer als trekt men de haan een paar maal over, gelijk moet er dan met de hak van rechterschoen (dame linker) een tikkend geluid op de vloer gemaakt worden . . . . Q Q S
1 maat

Na de 8ste maat weer, bij de 1e maat beginnen totaal 16 maten.

Nu in de Rumba houding een draai rechtsom dansen.

L. vt. voorwaarts . . . . Slow
L. vt. achterwaarts . . . . Slow
R. vt. achterwaarts . . . . Slow
R. vt. voorwaarts . . . . Slow
L. vt. voorwaarts . . . . Slow
L. vt. achterwaarts . . . . Slow
R. vt. achterwaarts . . . . Slow
R. vt. voorwaarts . . . . Slow

FIG. 4 — 8 MATEN

L. vt. voorwaarts . . . . Slow
L. vt. achterwaarts . . . . Slow
R. vt. achterwaarts . . . . Slow
R. vt. voorwaarts . . . . Slow
L. vt. voorwaarts . . . . Slow
L. vt. achterwaarts . . . . Slow
R. vt. achterwaarts . . . . Slow
R. vt. voorwaarts . . . . Slow
Beiden roepen nu „STOP"!!! 8 maten

FIG. 1 — 3 MATEN

L. vt. Voorwaarts (Trucking-walk) . . . . Q Q
R. vt. Voorwaarts „ „ . . . . Q Q
L. vt. Voorwaarts „ „ . . . . Q Q
R. vt. Voorwaarts „ „ . . . . Q Q
Op deze laatste pas een kwartdraai rechtsom dame linksom, zoo dat dame en heer nu met de gezichten naar elkaar toe staan.
L. vt. zijwaarts . . . . Slow
R. vt. herplaatsen . . . . Slow
3 maten

FIG. 2 — 1 MAAT

Dame en heer met linkerhand boven de oogen.
Heer naar rechts kijken, dame naar links kijken Slow
Heer naar links kijken, dame naar rechts kijken Slow
1 maat

FIG. 1 — 2 MATEN

L. vt. voorwaarts (Trucking-walk) . . . . . Q Q
R. vt. voorwaarts . . . . Q Q
op deze pas een kwartdraai rechtsom maken dame links om.
L. vt. zijwaarts . . . . Slow
R. vt. het gewicht er op terug laten komen . Slow
2 maten

FIG. 2 — 1 MAAT

Met de linkerhand boven de oogen naar rechts kijken de dame naar links . . . . Slow
Met linkerhand boven de oogen naar de dame er de dame naar den heer kijken . . . . . Slow
1 maat

FIG. 5 — 1 MAAT

De beweging maken als heeft men een sten-gun in aanslag. De dame zal nu haar handen in de hoogte doen als geeft zij zich over. De heer maakt dan met de hak van de rechterschoen weer het tikkende geluid . . . . Q Q S
1 maat

Totaal 32 maten

Dit is het einde van de dans totaal 32 maten, hij kan nu voor heer met L. vt. en dame met R. vt. herhaald worden.

DANSSCHOOL PIERRE ZOM Jr. - 's-GRAVENDIJKWAL 130 - TELEF. 32119
AUTEUR EN ONTWERPER VAN GEZELSCHAPSDANS „LES PETITS OISEAUX 1942 en DE STEN-GUN WALK 1945.

Dance instructions for *De Sten-Gun-Walk* performances on the back of the sheet music edition (1945). These illustrations resemble the traditions of dance instructions on sheet music like the ones of the edition of *Underneath the Chestnut Tree*, the British 'dance sensation' from 1939.

To give us freedom again.
Wave flags and pennants now high in the wind,
Where at last, God is praised,
Oppression is crushed and freedom begins.
And long live, long live the Canadians![58]

Another excellent example of Dutch gratitude towards the Canadian liberators is the *Canuck-Song* by composer Kees Sommer. The emotions reflected in the lyrics are predominantly those of joy, relief, and deep gratitude. The song recounts the liberation of Holland on May 9 in 1945, marking the end of Nazi occupation. This date is described as the 'brightest' and a 'golden day', underscoring its significance in Dutch history. The imagery of the 'rising of the long-expected freedom star' evokes a profound sense of liberation and newfound hope. The lyrics convey a strong sense of national pride and unity as the Dutch people collectively celebrate their freedom. The reference to the 'smiling Canuck' (a Canadian soldier) embodies the gratitude felt towards the Canadian forces for their pivotal role in securing this victory. The emotions expressed are a mix of jubilation, admiration, and thankfulness for the liberation and the end of a dark chapter in history.

The Dutch version of the lyrics carries an even more immediate and vibrant tone, capturing the lively atmosphere and the excitement of seeing the Canadian forces in action. It includes colloquial expressions like 'Hou Zee!' (the Hou rallying cry, meaning 'Hold steady') and 'moffen' (meaning 'Krauts') along with vivid descriptions of the events. The presence of the Canadian forces is portrayed in dynamic terms, with references to their swift actions, fast cars, and overall efficiency. The Dutch version also adopts a more communal perspective, inviting others to join in the celebration and witness the actions of the Canadian forces together.

A golden day stays in my memory:
'The 9th of May of nineteenhundred forty-five.'
That is the day that brought us liberty
That happy day by far the brightest of my life.
't Was the rising of the long expected freedom star.
Never Holland was so merry and so gay,
Then the world could state

Canuck-Song, cover (1945)

how 'cool' the silent Dutchmen are.
And from all the population I can say:
A golden day stays in my memory:
'The 9th of May of nineteenhundred forty-five.'

Then we saw the Canuck
He had a smile,
That seemed to say: Good luck.
Through the smiling Canuck
We knew that Hitler-Germany was 'stuk' [Dutch for broken, gone to pieces]
O, dear Canuck, your Canadian name
Is synonym [sic] with glory and fame!
Yes, we had good luck,
The day we met with our new friend 'The Canuck'[59]

The cover art cleverly combines visual metaphors to illustrate international encounters, while the accompanying text clearly conveys the song's theme. It features elements of Dutch cultural heritage, such as a large windmill in a rural setting, alongside jeeps speeding past a marching soldier whose oversized boot symbolizes leadership and determination. Scattered flowers along the path evoke a sense of beauty and renewal, ready to be embraced after the liberation. Above the title *Canuck-Song*, the publisher and lyricist have included a dedication: 'This March is dedicated to the Canadian Troops in Holland, May 1945.'

These songs often highlight the attraction Dutch women felt toward Canadian soldiers, as seen in *Het moet een Canadees zijn*, where composer Van Rido and lyricist Herbert Nelsen craft a chorus for Dutch girls singing, 'I'm in love with the First Canadian Army!' Similarly, Joop de Leur's foxtrot *Mijn Tommy uit Canada* (My Tommy from Canada) and Dutchie's flirtatious song *Little Holland Girl* depict romantic encounters with Canadian soldiers. In *Little Holland Girl*, a Canadian soldier in a jeep greets a 'little Holland girl', as the title suggests, in exchange for a tulip. This song, too, is dedicated to the Allied forces.

However, after the 'magical summer of liberation' in 1945, the narrative shifted from heroic tales to the more complicated realities of war, liberation, and occupation, which stirred mixed feelings among the Dutch. As Rense Havinga explains, complaints began to surface about Canadian soldiers occupying Dutch homes and engaging in black market activities. In a country in desperate need of currency reform, cigarettes became the most reliable form of exchange, and Canadian soldiers had them in abundance. Some soldiers, bored and restless, turned to excessive partying and instigating evening fights.[60]

With around 170,000 soldiers stationed in the Netherlands, the spread of sexually transmitted diseases became a significant concern, as did the increasing number of single mothers unable to maintain relationships with Canadian soldiers. Conservative estimates suggest that about 5,000 illegitimate children were born to Dutch women involved with Allied soldiers, though some sources claim the number could be as high as 8,000. In a society where single motherhood was still heavily stigmatized, this situation caused considerable distress. As Havinga states in his contribution to this book, a popular postwar joke captured the sentiment: 'If another war starts in 20 years, the Canadians won't need to send an army; a ship full of uniforms will suffice.'[61]

Young Dutch men, meanwhile, found their self-esteem severely undermined as they struggled to compete for attention with the young, heroic Allied liberators in uniform. It is not surprising that the mood among the Dutch population began to shift rapidly. This change is reflected in songs published later in 1945, which feature warnings, accusations, and ridicule, such as *Dag Sjaan, dag Bep, dag Alida*, *De Canadeesche Koorts*, and *Meisje, let op je zaak*.[62]

Jan Hendriks, who was nineteen years old at the end of WWII and performed for Allied soldiers in the Nijmegen concert hall, noted in his diary that Canadian soldiers often relieved their pre-battle stress with drinks the night before and frequently exhibited loose morals among the local population. His diary captures the mood of the time and the complexities of Canadian–Dutch interactions, particularly the Canadians' interest in Dutch girls and the struggles of young Dutch men to compete for their attention. On November 21, 1944, Hendriks wrote:

Nijmegen is a Catholic, conservative bulwark, but at present the clergy has no grip on this unexpected, new situation. We read in the papers that the

Nijmegen girls must preserve their honor, but there is no way that going out with Canadian soldiers or visiting dance parties can be forbidden. The population will not keep to the regulations. This is not a good time to be engaged to a Dutch girl. Many engagements are broken. The girls go out dancing with the Allied soldiers, and the Nijmegen boys have nothing to offer. The soldiers give the girls cigarettes, chocolate, and nylon stockings, a product we did not know yet. Dresses are made out of parachute materials, and the soldiers stationed in the Nijmegen area bring goods from empty houses in the frontlines and present these to the girls.[63]

In a similarly realistic manner, Canadian poet Earle Birney painted a less flattering picture of the Canadian liberators than many recalled from the early phase of enthusiasm during the liberation. Birney cautioned that Nazi propaganda had, to a certain painful degree, been accurate in predicting that the liberators would eventually exploit their situation.

You'll know them by their faces
Painted red, blue and yellow,
From the way they loot your houses,
Steal your food, rape your women
So keep your blinds well down,
Don't show fire-smoke,
Hide your daughters in the attic,
And perhaps do some extra praying.[64]

This description, however, presents an overly negative perspective and does not reflect the views of many in the Dutch population. During their time in the liberated southeast of the Netherlands, Canadian soldiers generally enjoyed a warm and friendly relationship with the local community and were widely welcomed as liberators. Despite occasional negative incidents, such as looting, black market activities, and other unfortunate experiences, the overall sentiment toward the Canadians remained positive. Historian Michael Horn noted that the Canadians were 'mostly young men who had fought, faced death, and lived', which helps explain their commendable behavior.[65]

The lighthearted approach to intercultural encounters took a bittersweet turn when nearly 2,000 so-called 'war brides' embarked on ships across the

Da-ag, Da-ag, Da-ag, cover (1945)

ocean, seeking a better life beyond the war-torn ruins of the Netherlands.[66] The Canadian government covered not only the passage for the Dutch women but also for at least 428 children to Canada.[67] Many others would soon follow, emigrating to join their sweethearts in Great Britain or the United States. However, because Canadian soldiers remained in the Netherlands for more than a year, they sometimes became the focal point of intercultural tensions.

Goodbye Tommie, cover (1945)

For some, the departure of these attractive soldiers was a source of sorrow, as reflected in the lyrics of *Goodbye Tommie* by Arnold Frank: 'Goodbye Tommie, / Goodbye Tommie, / De wereld weet nu wat je kan / Zelfs onder slijk en modder / Blijf je nog een gentleman.' (Goodbye Tommie, / Goodbye Tommie, / The world now knows what you can do / Even under mire and mud / You still remain a gentleman.) Yet, before many of these songs could be recorded and solidified in cultural memory, the magic of 1945 had already begun to fade.[68]

7
I CANNOT SWING:
LIBERATION BOOGIE-WOOGIE AND SWING

In contrast to the rigid, militaristic esthetics of marching promoted by the National Socialists and the NSB, the African American genre of boogie-woogie—and the emerging swing movement—emphasized individual vitality and expression through dance, rather than paramilitary drills accompanied by a steady beat. Boogie-woogie, primarily piano-based and characterized by its distinctive melodic bass lines and syncopated rhythms, gained widespread popularity in the 1930s and was embraced by swing

Gee, I Like This Boogey Woogey Swing, cover (1945)

bands like those of Tommy Dorsey and Glenn Miller. In the Netherlands, Hans Ninaber's 1945 song *Gee, I Like This Boogey Woogey Swing* exemplifies the transformative power of music in uplifting spirits and countering despair in postwar Netherlands.

Heeft U weleens zorgen?	There is a brand new rhythm,[69]
Last van rheumatiek...?	Listen for a while.
Dan weet ik een middel	To the very popular
't middel heet muziek:	Boogie-woogie style.
Speel voor mij een beetje dansmuziek.	Gee! I like that boogie-woogie swing
Daar ben ik dol op,	With boogie-woogie
Ja dat vind ik knal.	Life is never blue.

There is a subtle difference in emphasis between the Dutch and English lyrics of the song. The Dutch version more starkly contrasts the experience of grief with the healing power of boogie-woogie: 'met wat Boogey Woogey "Swing" muziek vind ik het leven lang nog niet zoo mal' (with this boogie-woogie swing music, I find life isn't so bad after all).[70] The transatlantic connection is vividly encapsulated on the cover, where a black-and-white illustration depicts Glenn Miller holding a musician with a trumpet in his arms, cradled like a small child. The imagery is highly symbolic, evoking

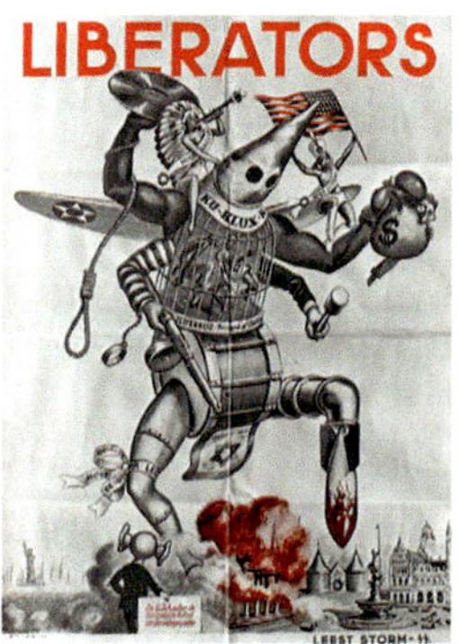

Poster for the exhibition 'Entartete Musik' (degenerate music) and two book covers of Dutch marching music of the Dutch National Socialist Movement, NSB

a paternal relationship between Miller and the figure he supports. To a Dutch audience, the implication would have been unmistakable: Glenn Miller serves as a father figure, a cultural icon whose music carries the promise of rejuvenation and vitality. His work embodies the spirit of liberation, signifying a fresh infusion of energy and hope into Dutch life after the hardships of occupation and war. This visual metaphor underscores the broader cultural and emotional significance of transatlantic influences in shaping postwar identity and aspirations in the Netherlands.

The National Socialists responded to performances by African American musicians and music rooted in Black culture with harsh defamation. The 1938 Düsseldorf exhibition *Entartete Musik* (Degenerate Music) labeled blues, boogie-woogie, and swing as poisonous infiltrations of so-called Aryan art.

The Dutch version of the National Socialist caricature of 'Kulturterror' (Cultural Terror)—a two-color version also published under the title 'Liberators'—encouraged viewers to read the Dutch Nazi paper *Storm SS* (see Illustration on the following page). The cover portrays the United States as a racist robot out of control, draped in a Ku Klux Klan hood, with a torso resembling a cage in which an African American couple dances the jitterbug, and legs made of bombs poised to destroy iconic German cities. Musically, the imagery discredits the U.S. as a nation wielding a gun in one hand and a drumstick in the other, ready to produce the rhythm of destruction. The perceived threat is further symbolized by the American war machine's weapons: a sack of dollars and a record, indicating the dangerous alliance between entertainment and capital. Overwhelmed by this 'acoustic terror', a small figure in the foreground can hardly believe his ears, which have grotesquely grown in size. The sign he holds sarcastically mocks the promise of liberation: 'De U.S.A. zullen de Europeesche Kultuur van den ondergang redden' (The United States will save European culture from destruction).[71]

As music scholar Walter van de Leur reminds us, concerns about the influence of American jazz on Dutch youth began long before the National Socialists occupied the Netherlands in May 1940. As early as 1931, Dutch politics was already wary of the allegedly subversive power of jazz, with modern dances like the foxtrot, shimmy, and charleston described as highly sexualized music that could test young people's morals.[72]

National Socialist Propaganda poster 'Kulturterror' aimed at Dutch audiences

Despite efforts by authorities, the spread of African American music in Germany and the Netherlands proved difficult to suppress.[73] By the time of the 1936 Olympic Games in Berlin, musical boundaries had already begun to blur. The sophisticated arrangements of orchestral dance music by artists like Duke Ellington and Benny Goodman impressed German musicians, who eagerly adopted the African American styles of swing, foxtrot, and boogie-woogie. German bandleaders like Teddy Stauffer and Kurt Widmann became prominent followers of Ellington and Goodman. As a result, swing sounds began to emerge from German record stores, movie theaters showing American musicals, and dance parties that featured music from both sides of the Atlantic.

However, due to the National Socialists' defamation of jazz and swing, the lyrics of 'hot music' were often Germanized. For instance, one of the earliest African American hits, *Tiger Rag*, was renamed *Schwarzer Panther*.[74] The National Socialists' approach to African American music was inconsistent—swing was alternately discredited as 'degenerate' or silently condoned.[75] This hypocrisy stemmed from the fact that the individualistic emphasis on solo instruments, improvisation, and African American roots did not align with the Nazi ideal of music as a tool for molding individuals into a uniform mass. Consequently, the German swing movement, with its creative, individualistic, and even anarchic attitude—complete with its own fashion code—became the first German youth subculture to define its resistance to the status quo through music.

Hans Dieter Schaefer described this ambivalence toward swing as a 'split conscience', a phenomenon that also emerged in the Netherlands. Swing and boogie-woogie could only be enjoyed when disguised under Dutch-sounding titles. One of the best known Dutch orchestras, The

Ramblers, was formed in 1926 (see Swart 233). They gained popularity in the wake of European tours by the famous African American clarinet player Sidney Bechet and Paul Whiteman, the self-proclaimed 'King of Jazz'. After 1933, The Ramblers became influential through their jazz and swing performances on VARA radio, *Vereeniging van Arbeiders Radio Amateurs* (Association of Worker Radio Amateurs). However, when in 1942 the *Departement van Volksvoorlichting en Kunsten* passed the law 'Verbod van negroide en negritische elementen in dans- en amusementsmuziek' (Law Against Black and 'Blackish' Influences in Dance and Popular Music), English-sounding band names were banned. The Ramblers were forced to rename themselves *Theo Uden Masman en zijn dansorkest*—Theo Uden Masman and His Dance Orchestra.

In the collective consciousness of the Netherlands, the sound and music of The Ramblers are closely tied to the soundtrack of liberation. Yet, in the summer of 1945, The Ramblers did not perform a single song from their jazz and swing repertoire within the country. Because they had also played for the German Wehrmacht and the National Socialist *Nederlandsch Arbeidersfront*, The Ramblers were banned from performing after the liberation. Under the leadership of drummer Kees Kranenburg, the band went on tour in other countries. After the magical summer of 1945, things calmed down, and in January 1946, the ban was lifted, allowing The Ramblers to continue their success.

The German term *Verniggerung* became part of a widespread prohibition of African American music in record stores and on radio stations during the war. African American performers were banned from Germany and the occupied countries, creating a musical vacuum in the Netherlands, as elsewhere. This vacuum explains the keen interest of Dutch music publishers and performers in gaining access to sheet music. However, printed scores alone could not capture the unique qualities of boogie-woogie, particularly its improvisational nature in live performances.

Early efforts by Dutch composers to incorporate these new genres were a form of musical appropriation, similar to the early experiments with jazz by Ernst Krenek, Erwin Schulhoff, Paul Hindemith, and Kurt Weill immediately after World War I. For example, the Dutch liberation song *Ik kan niet swingen* (I Cannot Swing) highlights the gap between the desire to participate in the new musical dance sensation from the U.S. and the inability to do so shortly after the liberation. Ironically, *Ik kan niet swingen* is composed as a foxtrot. As Duke Ellington famously said in 1932: 'It don't mean a thing if it ain't got that swing.'

'k kom uit heel gegoede kringen,	I come from high society,
'k kweek exotische seringen.	I grow exotic lilacs.
Ik zit vol betoveringen,	I am full of enchantments,
maar helaas, ik kan niet swingen.	But alas, I cannot swing.

The demand for jazz, swing, and blues persisted despite the differing tastes of the occupiers. Dutch musicians often found ingenious ways to continue playing their American-influenced repertoire while simultaneously appeasing—or outwitting—National Socialist regulators. Marcel Thielemans, trombonist for The Ramblers, recalled how they responded to the cultural restrictions: 'We were not allowed to play American songs. Of course, we played American songs, but we changed the titles. *Jazz Me Blues* became *Mijn Blauwe Jas* (My Blue Coat)... *Steeplechase* was *Hinternisrennen*, and so on.'[76]

Some songs took on different meanings depending on the listener's national and cultural background. For example, Jack Bulterman's slow foxtrot *Morgen komt een nieuwe dag* (Tomorrow Will Be a New Day) had to be submitted to the National Socialist Chamber of Culture before release, with a direct German translation, 'Morgen kommt ein neuer Tag'. The authorities overlooked any potential political subtext, but for Dutch listeners, the song conveyed an optimistic hope for a future free from Nazi occupation—a future where the occupiers would be driven out, court-martialed, and the Netherlands liberated.[77]

Morgen komt een nieuwe dag, cover (1943)

Ik kan niet swingen, score (1945)

Similarly, other songs acquired subversive undertones. The hit tune from the 1943 revue *Tok...Tok...Tok...Alweer Een Ei*, which included the line 'Als op het Leidscheplein de lichtjes weer eens branden gaan' (When the lights at Leidseplein shine again), described the anticipation of Am-

Als op het Leischeplein de lichtjes weer eens branden gaan, cover (1949)

sterdam's nightlife returning to its former glory, particularly at Leidseplein, a well-known entertainment venue.

However, the Nazi *Reichskommissariat Niederlande* became aware of the continued performances of non-German songs, leading to complaints and even warnings. On September 9, 1942, The Ramblers were threatened with a performance ban: 'The *Reichskommissariat* reports that you gave a concert in Arnhem that strongly hinted at English jazz. You also played too many French songs and only a few German ones. You must play many more German songs, or we will take measures.'[78] Jazz quickly evolved into a politically charged and polarizing cultural phenomenon. This was important for the Dutch musical landscape considering the limited availability of visiting American jazz musicians during the first five years after the end of World War II.[79]

8
SNOEZEPOES:
COMPOSING AND ARRANGING LIBERATION SONGS

Among the most successful Ramblers tunes after 1945 was Bulterman's composition *Bouncin' in Bavaria,* which became a standard in big band repertoires.[80] The song gained widespread recognition and was even hailed as the highlight of a concert in Groningen in February 1950. In Great Britain, *Bouncin' in Bavaria* was one of the most requested songs (Morley 131). The American Forces Network (AFN) in Munich adopted it as the signature tune for their radio show of the same name, further solidifying its popularity. An article in *Nieuwsblad van het Noorden* highlighted the song's association with AFN, describing it as 'the well-known AFN tune'.[81] This connection between a Dutch swing tune celebrating liberation and the cultural memory of the AFN radio audience in Germany illustrates how music can transcend national boundaries, even if its origins aren't always recognized.

Jack Bulterman, born on September 27, 1909 in Amsterdam, was a multi-talented musician—composer, pianist, trumpeter, and accordionist—who became a key figure in the genre of liberation songs.[82] After joining The Ramblers in 1935, he composed popular foxtrots, blues, swing, and later twist dances, often with English lyrics. The band's extensive touring made them well-known even among German audiences. In addition to composing, arranging, and performing jazz, Bulterman wrote lyrics for many hits.

The five-year German occupation of the Netherlands between May 1940 and May 1945 forced significant changes in the Dutch jazz repertoire to diminish so-called 'negroid' elements. Ironically, the occupation spurred a creative surge among Dutch musicians and composers as the British and American markets for popular music became less accessible.[83] Dutch composers began producing dance songs for radio, cabaret, dance halls, revues, and cafés in unprecedented numbers (Swart 229). After the liberation, the Dutch music scene became more international again, allowing Bulterman to explore a wider variety of styles and reconnect with contemporary American musical trends.

Bulterman had been attuned to musical developments in the United States and the latest ballroom dances in Great Britain from early on. When the first American dance records became available on the Dutch market after World War I, bands like Art Hickman's New York London Five toured the country, paving the way for Dutch bands like the Original Victoria Band and Dick Willebrandts' orchestra. Along with amateur jazz performers like Ernst van 't Hoff, Melle Weersma, and Jack de Vries, they introduced a fresh sound to the Netherlands. As a result, traditional German songs, Viennese waltzes, tangos, and operetta melodies quickly became outdated.[84] With Duke Ellington, Louis Armstrong, Cab Calloway, and Paul Whiteman touring, young Dutch people had ample opportunities to experience American jazz at venues like the Wanderers Hotclub in The Hague and the Nederlandsche Jazz Liga, or on the radio, particularly with The Ramblers serving as musical mediators for VARA radio as the official VARA Dance Orchestra. In 1931, the magazine *De Jazzwereld* (Jazz World) was founded and became an influential publication with a dual mission: to inform Dutch readers about cutting-edge musical developments and to 'defend jazz against the prejudices of its critics'.[85]

The postwar sheet music publication *Maa...rrr wij komen terug!* ('However, we are coming back'), a potpourri of hits of The Ramblers during the time before and after the occupation, has often been taken to suggest the orchestra's return to the music scene.[86] In truth, The Ramblers' music, with Jack Bulterman's arrangements, had never really disappeared. Songs

Maa...rrr wij komen terug!, cover

like *Meisje, je vous aime beaucoup*, *Wat 's nachts de bloemen fluist'ren*, *Wie is Loesje?*, *Ik kan je niet vertellen*, *Rosie*, *Hocus-Pocus-Pa's*, *Roosmarie*, *Een ogenblikje stilte*, *Oh Marjanka*, *Dag*, *Schatteboutje*, *Schenk mij je glimlach Marietje*, and *De zon gaat weer schijnen*—as well as songs with German

Dag, Schatteboutje, cover (1931)

lyrics like *Tanzmusik* and *Ach, Fräulein Gretchen!* (the German version of *Dag, Schatteboutje*, 1940)—were all part of their war repertoire.

The cover of *Maa…rrr wij komen terug!* features a caricature of The Ramblers, with what appears to be Jack Bulterman at the center, playing the saxophone.[87] The subtitle 'Arrangements by Jack Bulterman' underscores Bulterman's pivotal role in the production of hit records during those years. Notably, the cover also includes the image of an African American musician, likely representing U.S. saxophonist Coleman Hawkins, who played and recorded with The Ramblers in the 1930s. This depiction of an African American presence suggests a direct connection to the United States, lending a sense of authenticity to Bulterman's successful jazz compositions.

Bulterman's songs became central to the short-lived genre of liberation songs. Drawing on his work with The Ramblers, where he played the trumpet and served as an arranger from 1935 to 1946, he incorporated cabaret elements into the experience of liberation between 1944 and 1945. A photograph of an advertisement in the front window of an Amsterdam music shop suggests that the types of liberation songs he composed were in high demand in 1945.[88]

The collection *Maa…rrr wij komen terug!* offers a fruitful scholarly opportunity to explore, describe, and hear the soundtrack of liberation in a collection of Dutch compositions that celebrate the feeling of 'being free again', rather than in a mere medley of American or British success hits. With these musical notes and lyrics captured on paper, we hold the key to get closer to answering the questions of what kind of music was played, what kind of songs were sung, and what kind of dances were performed in the summer of 1945.[89]

Many of the songs address the exciting atmosphere of intercultural encounters between Dutch people and the Allied forces from Canada, the United

Kingdom, and the United States. In a lighthearted manner, they make fun of cultural misunderstandings or language problems. Examples include Jack Millar's *White Stripes in a Sky of Blue*, or Jack Bulterman's foxtrot *Snoezepoes*. The case of *Snoezepoes* shows that Bulterman's song from 1940, five years before the liberation, gained new currency in the political environment. The tune was popular both as sheet song and on Dutch radio as mentioned on the cover. Here, a scenario of romantic encounters from the time of occupation (in the German context between a Nazi soldier and a Dutch girl) could be successfully transferred to the period of Dutch liberation as an encounter between a liberator and a Dutch girl. The reference to 'German Words: Hanns Kunz' suggests that the song also appealed to German occupiers.

The song pays tribute to stereotypes of Dutch culture familiar to Americans through songs like Bing Crosby's interpretation of *Little Dutch Mill*, which was a number one hit in 1934, or Glenn Miller's popular tune *In an Old Dutch Garden (By an Old Dutch Mill)* from 1939. The song *Snoezepoes*, composed in 1940, even quotes the title of the Miller hit almost verbatim in the first line: 'By the old Dutch mill we were sitting hand in hand.' The Allied soldier and the Dutch girl fall in love. Alas, neither one of the young lovers understands a single sentence: 'I whispered tender words that she did not understand.' The only word the soldier has learned and remembers lovingly is the Dutch expression for sweetheart—*snoezepoes*. Other intertextual references are related to Dutch stereotypes like the iconic old Dutch mill, wooden shoes, memories of first encounters with whispers of love (see lyrics below).

As W.J.T. Mitchell reminds us, there is no such thing as a pure medium. Instead, we should consider all media as 'mixed media' (211). Sheet music publications combine lyrics with the score and stylish cover art. The graphic design of *Snoezepoes* bears strong resemblance to *In an Old Dutch Garden (By an Old Dutch Mill)* by exaggerating national stereotypes. With monochromatic background colors of green and red respectively, both sheet music publications show simplistic drawings of a mill with an allegedly Dutch girl wearing an apron, a typical Dutch dress, and starched bonnets with wings on their heads. They also feature blond hair (at least in the American example) and the iconic wooden shoes. The comparison reveals how images and sounds travel and become reappropriated in different national contexts.

By an *old Dutch mill*
We were sitting hand in hand;
I *whispered* tender words,
That she didn't understand,
And I'll never forget,
Tho' the years passed away
The lovely word for 'sweetheart'
I learned that day:

'Snoezepoes!' Snoezepoes!
There by the *old Dutch mill*,
How I like your *wooden shoes*
And your *smile I remember* still!
I met her on a bench
Near a linden tree
And she said to me
That her heart was free...
Snoezepoes! Snoezepoes!
Little girl with your *wooden shoes*![90]

In an *old Dutch* garden
By an *old Dutch mill*,
Where the moon was dreaming
On a distant hill,
When a *smile* danced by
It was then that I saw
Heaven in a pair *of wooden shoes*.
In an *old Dutch* garden
Where the *tulips* grow
That's where *I first whispered*
That I love you so
For my *heart* was blue till I gave it to
An angel in a pair of *wooden shoes*.
Then one sad day
When summer meets September

Sheet music covers of *Snoezepoes* (The Hague: Muziek-Smith, 1940, republished 1945) by Jack Bulterman. The two publication dates indicate that Bulterman saw a chance to market his song both a German and later an international audience.

> I sailed away from a thrill
> I will *remember*.

The exhilarating experience of international and intercultural encounters in the summer of 1945 inspired a wealth of songs that humorously addressed the challenges of expressing emotions across cultures and language barriers. Dutch composers captured the unique atmosphere of that time with foxtrot tunes that drew on the musical styles they knew from before and during the war. Examples include *Geef mij maar 'n echt Hollandsch Meisje*, *Little Holland Girl*, *Mijn Tommy uit Canada*, and the popular *Trees heeft een Canadees*.

In addition to exploring intertextual, interpictorial, and intersonic themes, I will now focus on another key element that helped cross-pollinate jazz in a transnational context: radio broadcasts by the American Forces Network (AFN).

Little Holland Girl
60 ct
WORDS AND MUSIC
by „DUTCHIE"
DEDICATED TO THE ALLIED FORCES

9
BOUNCIN' IN BAVARIA: BROADCASTING DUTCH SWING IN OCCUPIED GERMANY

The success of Jack Bulterman and The Ramblers, both in and beyond the Netherlands, can be attributed to their ability to perform for an international audience across a wide range of musical genres. In contrast to Spain, Italy, or countries in Eastern Europe, the Netherlands lacks a distinctly identifiable folk music tradition. Instead, the country embraced what Aat Swart describes as a 'xenophilic musical culture',[91] evident in its popular music, which often blends styles, influences, and musical idioms from various cultural backgrounds.

Dutch composers and orchestras distinguished themselves through remarkable adaptability, often incorporating elements from Viennese *Lieder*, German marches, Spanish paso dobles, hillbilly songs, Hawaiian hulas, or Hungarian czardas into their compositions.[92] The Ramblers kept a close eye on the latest developments in jazz and tailored their performances to suit the mood of the times. By the 1950s, they could proudly claim to be 'the oldest dance orchestra in the world',[93] a title they still hold today, as confirmed by the Guinness Book of World Records. The bandleader, Theo Udo Masman, meticulously devised charts and statistics to develop musical programs that would resonate positively with audiences.[94]

Jack Bulterman's extensive body of work exemplifies his ability to adapt to popular tastes and incorporate emerging musical trends. Over several decades, Bulterman created songs in a variety of styles, including blues (*Zuyderzee Blues*, 1943), German dance music (*Dansmuziek/Tanzmusik*, 1940s), American swing (*Swing Me to Sleep, Drummer-man*, 1947), Dutch postwar cabaret (*Hallo, Hella, Hallo*, 1952), and American twist (*Clap Your Hands and Twist*, 1962). He was often credited with having a unique ability to quickly recognize and adapt to current trends, transforming them into exciting new songs.

The creation of *Wie is Loesje* (1939) is a prime example of Bulterman's creative process. He recounted:

'We were always looking for good songs in which Kees could play his percussion solos. An example of this was "Who is Loesje". I had thought

Little Holland Girl, cover (1945)

Clockwise: *Zuyderzee Blues*, cover: *Tanz Musik Dans Muziek*, cover; *Clap your hands and twist*, cover; *Ach, Fräulein Gretchen*, cover

Wie is Loesje?, cover (1939)

about a drum song and found a refrain that didn't seem very suitable, so I hadn't written it down for the orchestra. There was also a verse to go with it for which I sprang the words, "Who is Loesje!" and on impulse I realized that this had to be the chorus. "Who is Loesje? Who is that sweetie?" And then the whole orchestra: "Loesje is the girl of the band's drummer!" And further on, "Hear, there he just hit a break!" (Djieng-boom, djieng-djieng-djieng-boom!) "She feels a sting in her heart!" (Pats!)'[95]

Immediately after the end of World War II, Bulterman's light and joyful swing songs struck a chord among both Dutch citizens and liberators. In the Netherlands, jazz was no longer associated with the notion of sinful, primitive, uncivilized music. Rather, the cultural opposition towards the music of the German occupiers turned jazz into the soundtrack of the liberators. Syncopation, swing, blue notes, and improvisation became loaded with political associations. As Kees Wouters suggests, by objecting to jazz, Dutch people risked the stigma of siding with the former enemy: 'Playing a Nat Gonella or a Benny Goodman record on a birthday party, one demonstrated that one was on the 'right' side' ('Introduction' 507). The attitude towards jazz in the Netherlands would soon become more nuanced and polarized.[96] In 1945, Bulterman recognized an opportunity to fashion himself into a musical mediator par excellence.

After the end of World War II, Bulterman played with The Ramblers in Belgium for American troops. Among the most successful tunes was Bulterman's composition *Bouncin' in Bavaria*, which became a standard in big band repertoires[97] and gained recognition in many European countries. In Great Britain, *Bouncin' in Bavaria* was one of the most requested pieces, thanks to its appealing selection of songs.[98] The song was also a highlight of a concert in Groningen in February 1950, with an article in *Nieuwsblad van het Noorden* identifying it as a well-known AFN tune.[99] The association with the American Forces Network (AFN) radio invites further exploration from the conceptual perspective of intersonic clusters.

The AFN's mission in Germany was to establish studios in cities like Berlin, Bremerhaven, Frankfurt, Kaiserslautern, Munich, Nuremberg, Stuttgart, and Würzburg to entertain American soldiers and their families. After 1946, the AFN broadcast daily from 5 AM until 1 PM, featuring so-called V-discs (Victory Discs) imported directly from American radio stations. V-discs were government-issued records produced to entertain American troops stationed overseas during the war, allowing soldiers access to popular jazz, swing, and blues. Moderators, often imitating stereotypical American radio voices, presented popular music, blues, country, and jazz, and later rock and soul, to the American forces. When American stars performed in Germany, AFN frequently recorded and broadcast their shows. With *Bouncin' in Bavaria* as the signature tune for the AFN Munich radio show of the same name, the sound signature of an influential tune connecting young German audiences to jazz in the 1950s was, in fact, a Dutch composition.

The Ramblers in front of the AFN Studios in Munich, Dec. 1948. *Tuney Tunes*, Apr. 1949. Image provided courtesy of Ate van Delden, private archive

A photo from December 1948 shows The Ramblers orchestra in front of the AFN studio on Kaulbachstrasse in Munich, where they performed live on air. The show *Bouncin' in Bavaria* was broadcast daily from 5:05 to 5:50 PM between 1953 and 1956, meaning that by the time AFN first used the song as its opener, it was already seven years old.[100] Since AFN was established in order to create a special emotional link between American soldiers, who found themselves far from home in a different social and cultural environment, it is surprising that a Dutch composition could provide the illusion of 'feeling American'. The song was so popular that listeners protested when the programmers removed the show. It would not take long for *Bouncin' in Bavaria* to return to AFN (Bulterman 121). Given that AFN was established to create an emotional connection between American soldiers stationed far from home in a different cultural environment, it's surprising that a Dutch composition could evoke a sense of 'feeling American'. The song was so popular that listeners protested when it was removed from the program, prompting its swift return (Bulterman 121). By 1953, the number of letters AFN received from German listeners exceeded those from American audiences (Schäfers 311), suggesting that the signature song was particularly popular among Germans as well. This phenomenon must be understood in the context of jazz's appeal after World War II and the role of AFN radio in Western Germany.

For young German music lovers, tuning in to AFN represented a cultural experience radically different from the conventional German radio programming they were accustomed to, especially in light of the Nazi past. In 1952, *Der Spiegel* described the typical German radio style as follows: 'So far, the German radio listener has only been familiar with highly stilted dialogs between musical tunes or "official words". Strictly according to manuscript, if possible anonymous and impersonal' ('Heiß' 29; translation by the author)[101] However, the postwar jazz scene in Germany was not as vibrant as cultural memory might suggest. Jazz aficionado Horst Lange, who wrote the first history of jazz in postwar Germany, expressed disappointment with the American music broadcast by AFN:

'Whoever thought that jazz would come to Germany with the Americans would soon find out otherwise, especially if he was a serious jazz aficionado. He had to learn the hard way that the average American knew as much or as little about jazz as the average German. Most of the Americans or U.S. soldiers leaned towards hillbilly (cowboy) music, Hawaiian music, and cheap hits, comparable with the German penchant for sentimental schmalz and *Heimatlieder* (patriotic folk tunes). In general, anything presented as American music by various AFN stations was considered "jazz"' (Lange 145; translation by the author).

While Lange's account is emotionally charged, reflecting the perspective of a jazz enthusiast, other sources confirm that postwar views of American jazz were often 'ill-informed and superficial' (Willett 92). AFN's programming was diverse, with jazz competing alongside classical music and, most notably, country music (sometimes labeled 'hillbilly' or 'cowboy' music). A poll suggested that due to the large number of GIs from southern states, country music, particularly songs by Grandpa Jones and the Grand Ole Opry troupe—including famous musicians like Roy Acuff and Hank Williams—ranked among the most popular genres in Germany (see Willett 91).

Why did *Bouncin' in Bavaria* become such a hit on AFN Munich? Following the end of World War II, The Ramblers toured Belgium, particularly Brussels and Antwerp, where they played for American forces. Many GIs viewed the orchestra as an excellent U.S. Army band. The Ramblers recorded an impressive 50 records 'by permission of the American authorities' (Oudejans), among which *Bouncin' in Bavaria*, as indicated on the Decca

Last page of The Ramblers' arrangement for Glenn Miller's 'In the Mood' with fanfare at the end. Courtesy of Ramblers member Bert Paige (21).

Arrangements for The Ramblers Orchestra. Manuscript. No. 192714. Muziekschatten archive, Muziekbibliotheek van het Muziekcentrum van de Omroep

labels. It's clear that Bulterman chose the song to please his American audience, meeting their expectations for a lively swing tune.

Building on Glenn Miller's *In the Mood*, the iconic wartime swing tune, *Bouncin' in Bavaria* has a similarly dynamic structure while offering its unique stylistic innovations. Where Miller's composition culminates in a fanfare finale anchored in a chromatically rising horn section, Bulterman's piece opens with a three-bar exclamation in F minor at a mid-tempo pace. This introduction transitions seamlessly into a five-note chromatic motif, rhythmically punctuated by the snare drum, setting the stage for a vibrant swing arrangement. The introduction is repeated throughout the piece to separate

Opening fanfare of Jack Bulterman's 'Bouncin' in Bavaria' (Brussels: Bens, 1946) for trumpet

two different syncopated melodic lines. The second motif is clearly inspired by a Bavarian folk tune, followed by a third melody played by saxophones. With this song, Bulterman playfully riffs on Bavarian folk music and the arrival of American troops, much like the 'ragging the classics' trend in the United States during the 1910s. Bulterman applies this technique to Southern German folk dances within the swing genre. The song also appeared in Germany under the title *Swing im Oberland*, with a nod to the foxtrot genre. Published by Musikverlag Melodie in Berlin, the Dutch composer's joke about the American cultural invasion of Southern Germany becomes obscured—or even lost—within the German cultural context.

At the turn of the twentieth century, many American composers used European music, particularly opera, as material for burlesque musical theater. For instance, Irving Berlin's ragtime opera *Watch Your Step* (1914) infused operatic classics by Verdi, Bizet, Puccini, Gounod, and Leoncavallo with the syncopated rhythms of contemporary dance music (Magee 53). This 'ragging' technique allowed American composers and audiences to poke fun at the revered European art of opera. Similarly, Bulterman takes the second melodic phrase of a traditional Plattler dance like the 'Auerhahn Plattler' and injects syncopations to make the melody swing—or, as the title suggests, bounce. He transforms the original 3/4 rhythm into a syncopated 4/4 meter, closely following the melodic progression of the Plattler while assigning the original accordion sounds to a horn section composed of trumpet, trombone, and saxophone.

The term 'bouncing' or 'bounce' was commonly used to describe upbeat jazz tunes and became a hallmark of the bebop style popularized by Charlie Parker.[102] 'Bouncing' signified a lively jazz tempo. According to the Oxford English Dictionary, 'more bounce to the ounce' was a popular phrase at the time, and 'bounce' generally means 'to rebound from an impact', which has fitting connotations for the role of music in uplifting war-weary citizens in European cities ('Bounce'). In 1945, Charlie Parker's *Billie's Bounce* (dedicated to Billy Shaw) became a hit and was later inducted into the Grammy Hall of Fame in 2002. In the summer of 1946, the same year Bulterman composed *Bouncin' in Bavaria*, New York jazz pianist Bud Powell composed *Bouncin' with Bud*, which quickly became a jazz standard. A few years earlier, Fats Waller had musically commented on the V-disc practice of AFN with his number *Bouncin' on a V-disc*. These government-sponsored 12-inch Victory Discs were sent to U.S. overseas radio stations starting in 1943, the year the American Forces Network went on the air in Europe, to entertain the troops.

The fact that a 1946 song, composed in honor of the American liberators and as a token of Dutch admiration for American jazz as a symbol of newfound freedom, could become the signature tune for an AFN Munich jazz broadcast highlights the programmers' indifference to the national origins of musical compositions. This indifference highlights how postwar cultural exchanges blurred national boundaries, allowing Dutch compositions like *Bouncin' in Bavaria* to transcend their origins and become emblematic of American jazz's global influence.

AFN effectively transnationalized the song, presenting the Dutch take on German folk music as an American musical joke. This aligns with observations that German big bands often lagged behind the latest musical developments in the United States.[103] However, the American occupation forces favored European adaptations of American swing in the style of Glenn Miller's orchestra. The performances and recordings of The Ramblers in Munich demonstrate the enthusiasm of GIs for the orchestra, yet it is likely that most listeners were unaware of the song's Dutch origins. The Germanized title 'Swing im Oberland' further obscured the Dutch background and the musical joke.[104] The Ramblers' ability to seamlessly blend Dutch musical idioms with American jazz styles positioned them as key cultural mediators during a period of transatlantic musical exchange.

10
AMERICA, WE THANK YOU: CONSENT AND SATIRE

The public's hopeful vision of the future is vividly reflected in songs that express gratitude to the Allied forces. Cultural practices such as singing serve as indicators of how a nation and its citizens cope with moments of crisis. In 1945, Ar Colijn composed *The Bells Now Ring Again*, a sonic memorial of gratitude. After the war, the church bells that had survived Nazi requisition for war materiel returned to Dutch church towers, reminding citizens that these sounds heralded a new era of transatlantic friendship. It was a time to sing and be thankful. Colijn's lyrics specifically acknowledge the contributions of British and American soldiers: 'Let's elevate our voice, / sing to the Tommy boys / our songs of gratitude.' Another verse celebrates the newfound sense of freedom and camaraderie with America: 'Liberty!!! / Now shake hands, / with the Americans, / in steady brotherhood, / and cheery mood.'

United States cultural diplomacy sought to cultivate a lasting memory of gratitude toward the liberators. For example, the European Recovery Program emphasized clear, accessible messages about why the U.S. was supporting the economies of both former foes and allies. Launched in 1948, the Marshall Plan aimed to rebuild war-torn European economies, promote free-market systems, and forge political alliances during the early Cold War. Dutch artist Jo Spier effectively conveyed this narrative in the booklet *Het Marshall-Plan en U!* (*The Marshall Plan and You*, 1949), which combined short texts and visuals to promote the Marshall Plan and European cooperation to the Dutch public.[105]

In one striking cartoon, Spier illustrated the benefits of American aid with the caption: 'Zonder Marshall hulp kunnen de Schoorstenen niet meer roken / en u ook niet!' (Without Marshall aid, the chimneys cannot smoke / and neither can you!). Through this imagery, Spier became a persuasive agent of American public diplomacy, showing that the U.S. was not a threat to Dutch culture and independence but an essential ally for progress in the postwar climate of free-market and consumer-oriented exchange.

The cover of the booklet features a typical Dutchman from the idyllic fishing village of Volendam, wearing a traditional hat and pipe, climbing a ladder of success framed by the American dollar sign. This playful imagery suggests that embracing American support could enhance, rather than diminish, the Netherlands' economic future and cultural identity, provided

Jo Spier, cartoons from the booklet *The Marshall Plan and You*, 1949

the relationship was navigated wisely. This delicate balance between gratitude, consent, and both national and transnational agendas is also reflected in the music and cover art of liberation songs.

This approach by Dutch artists also found its way into songs like *Marshall Liedje* (1948) by Lou Bandy & The Ramblers. In the song, George C. Marshall, the architect of the European Recovery Program, is celebrated as a modern-day Sinterklaas whose 'financial presents' supposedly turned the country into one great party.

Marshall, Marshall/ Kom toch gauw
Want heel Europa zit aan lager wal
Marshall, Marshall
Kom ons helpen uit dat financiële tranendal
Oh, Sint Marshall kapoentje,
Kom gooi wat in m'n schoentje
Marshall, Marshall
Waar de dollars zijn, daar is het bal.

Marshall, Marshall
Come soon
For all Europe is down
Marshall, Marshall
Come help us out of that financial vale of tears
Oh, Saint Marshall Kapoentje,
Come throw some in my shoe
Marshall, Marshall
Wherever the Dollars are, it's a ball.[106]

While the song appears to celebrate the Marshall Aid, its ironic undertone—likely to escape American authorities—suggests that Dutch citizens were willing to be treated like children as long as the money kept coming in.[107] In a similar fashion, the song *America, We Thank You* from 1949 offers a mix of Dutch and English lyrics in the chorus. Should a listener be unfamiliar with the Dutch language, the only lines that would make sense are 'America, We Thank You' and 'Good old America'. On the surface, the chorus explains that the Dutch are grateful for all the good things that the U.S. did. Now, how-

America, We Thank You, cover (1949)

ever, it is time for the U.S. to stop treating the Netherlands like emasculated little children. The final line of the chorus is a command: 'Geef Holland toch "Vrij baan!"—Just give Holland a "free ride"!'[108] This reference to freedom, juxtaposed with the reliance on American financial support, echoes the imagery found in *The Marshall Plan and You*. The cover of this booklet depicts a Dutchman climbing a ladder shaped like a dollar sign, with a map of Europe patched with dollar symbols (see previous illustration).

The cover art of the *America, We Thank You* sheet music further reinforces these themes, featuring a stereotypical Dutch girl in a bonnet, holding tulips and standing in a field of flowers. Such imagery is common on the covers of liberation songs, with tulips particularly symbolizing the joy of regained freedom, as exemplified by William Blees's song *Tulips Bloom in Holland Once Again*.

> Tulips bloom in Holland once again
> People smile in Holland once again
> Sad hearts have brightened since our Victory
> All hard days now have gone for pleasant times
> and more: Liberty!
> Tulips bloom in Holland once again.

In *America, We Thank You*, a young girl stands in front of a field of tulips, expressing her gratitude to a towering Uncle Sam, who looms against a backdrop of modern skyscrapers. Like a protective father figure, Uncle Sam firmly grasps the girl's right hand while shielding her over her head with his other hand. In return for his guidance, she offers him a bouquet of tulips. The cover art communicates a dual meaning steeped in both consent and satire: on one level, the Netherlands is portrayed as a daughter to the American paternal figure, with America cast as the wise and superior guide. On another level, the imagery hints at the Dutch willingness to accept American stereotypes of Dutchness, as long as tangible benefits—like postwar aid—are provided. Dutch citizens were certainly aware that the Marshall Plan served as a vehicle for advancing U.S. cultural interests abroad. This ambivalence toward American soft power illustrates how popular music, in the sense described by Stuart Hall, becomes an arena where consent and resistance are negotiated in the struggle over cultural meanings.

11
AS TIME GOES BY: JAZZ AS A LINGUA FRANCA

An intersonic reading of Bulterman's songs reveals the fluidity and potential of resignifying jazz across various cultural, national, and media contexts, including sheet music and radio broadcasts. The Dutch foxtrot *Snoezepoes* and the swing number *Bouncin' in Bavaria* exemplify how intersonic clusters operate within a multi-layered, palimpsestic media environment. Intersonic clusters refer to the interplay of sonic elements across cultural and media contexts, emphasizing music's ability to carry shared meanings beyond national boundaries. When combined with visual culture studies, these intersonic readings enhance our understanding of how jazz emerged and functioned within a transnational imaginary of 'America'. This leads us to a surprising conclusion: Jack Bulterman's jazz creates a musical bridge between the country liberated by the United States and that of the occupiers and oppressors.

Jazz, as a transnational lingua franca, served as a veiled form of self-Americanization, detached from the essentialist notion of jazz as exclusively 'Black' music. However, what various national audiences associated with this musical language—and what they sought to express through it—varied significantly. For instance, while Cornel West describes the struggle for freedom as central to African American music, in the Netherlands, Dutch swing and foxtrot tunes symbolized the successful struggle for liberation from occupation and foreign cultural control. Similarly, in Germany, young audiences turned to the jazzy soundtrack of liberation, broadcast via American radio stations, to cultivate a sense of freedom—decades before President Richard

Tulips bloom in Holland once again, cover (1945)

von Weizsäcker redefined 'Zero hour' as a time marked by the values of freedom rather than defeat. Although May 8th was not a day for celebration, it was, as Weizsäcker declared, 'a day of liberation. It liberated all of us from the inhumanity and tyranny of the National Socialist regime' (Weizsäcker, 1985).

In postwar Western Germany, this opportunity to re-embrace the values of freedom and democracy also led to a transnational appropriation of the latest developments in American music, paralleling the responses in the Netherlands after liberation. In 1945 and the following years, jazz emerged as a resignified element in a transnational contact zone where national residues were obscured, blurred, or even fictionalized. This musical soundtrack, functioning as a lingua franca, transported the feelings of freedom and liberation across both sides of the German–Dutch border—from the streets of Amsterdam to the homes of German shadow audiences tuning in to AFN in Munich—but with a significant twist. AFN's broadcasts served as cultural diplomacy, blending American values with the allure of jazz, fostering transatlantic connections and introducing jazz to European audiences.

The cultural and sonic imaginary 'America' was intertwined with a national fantasy of democratic success, perhaps even linked to and evolving from the African American struggle for equality in the United States. Yet, as illustrated by *Bouncin' in Bavaria*, this fantasy ultimately became part of a transnational imagery, filtered through the Dutch experience of cultural occupation, trauma, and liberation. In this context, The Ramblers emerged as unofficial jazz ambassadors in Germany via the American Forces Network. The Dutch liberation song, born from the experience of occupation, was resignified as part of Germany's musical liberation after World War II.

Sheet music for liberation songs initially served as a cherished means of celebrating newfound freedom through scores, lyrics, and striking images. However, soon after the war, another medium—radio—began to transform how Dutch people experienced music. Many of those I spoke to vividly remember learning and enjoying new songs by listening to the radio, even as memories of sheet music have faded. The song *Hilversum I* emphasizes the power of radio to provide a renewed sense of hope and freedom through musical broadcasts.

Hilversum I, cover (1954)

Nederlandsche Omroep geeft vrolijkheid en kleur
en brengt, via den aether, U in een goed humeur!
De Nederlandsche Omroep biedt uit zijn repertoire
al wat U maar kunt wensen en staat ook
nu voor mij en U weer klaar.

Dutch radio gives cheer and color
and, through the ether, puts you in a good mood!
The Nederlandsche Omroep offers from its repertoire
all you could wish for and is
now ready for me and you.[109]

The lyrics by Anton Beuving also indicate what kind of music was played: theater, music, entertainment in radio plays and revues. The ramblers were particularly popular and played many songs from the time before the war and new ones—including some that were only available as sheet music in the remarkable summer of 1945.

Nearly 80 years after the end of WWII, it's easy to take the values of freedom, democracy, open borders, and peace in the European Union for granted. While a shared generation's 'passion for American culture' once served as a unifying force for the European Union, recent polls reveal a growing disenchantment with the United States. Martha Bayles described this as the 'slow death of public diplomacy', which has led to contradictions, misunderstandings, and estrangement. Now is an opportune moment to explore the power of music as a unifying force between people and nations, especially in times of crisis. I'd like to share a personal experience of transatlantic sonic diplomacy and gratitude.

The Dutch architect Jan Hendriks (1925-2017) was one of the young pianists who, at the age of 19, played popular American songs like *As Time Goes By*, *Body and Soul*, *Blue Skies*, *I Can't Give You Anything But Love*, *I'll Get By*, *Lady Be Good*, *The Man I Love*, *Mood Indigo*, and *In the Mood* for Allied soldiers after the city of Nijmegen was liberated during Operation Market Garden in the fall of 1944.[110]

Jan Hendriks emphasized that Dutch songs, particularly the upbeat compositions by The Ramblers, were popular among both the Dutch and

Pianist Jan Hendriks (left) in the Vereeniging concert hall in Nijmegen

the Allied soldiers. Songs that resonated during the war included *Als Sterren Flonkerend aan de Hemel Staan*, *Een zonnig Madeira*, *Dag Schatteboutje*, and *Ouwe Taaie*. Hendriks confirmed that Jack Bulterman's music was especially beloved, with the famous big band performing at the Vereeniging concert hall in Nijmegen once or twice a year. When playing for the Allied soldiers, Jan Hendriks and his band primarily performed two types of songs: 'There were great songs from America by composers like Cole Porter, for example, and others. But those were melancholy songs—*I'll Be Seeing You*, *Sentimental Journey*... We played two kinds actually, that swing interspersed with those soft, say melancholy songs—*I'll Get By*, and *As Time Goes By*, we played that too.'[III]

The Dutch band's performances of classic American songs from the Great American Songbook tradition symbolized a new beginning for the Netherlands. For the soldiers, the music evoked memories of home, providing comfort and a boost in morale as they found themselves far from loved ones in a foreign land. Reflecting on those times, Hendriks recognized the central role of music during war and liberation.

Well into his 80s, Hendriks continued to play these songs in bars, museums, and other public venues. He shared his memories with audiences, both young and old, reminding them of music's enduring power. These concerts became transatlantic performances of gratitude and living mem-

Foxtrots.

1. Who's sorr[illegible].(B♭).
2. Whistling.(F.).
3. Rosetta.(F.).
4. Take the A-train.(B♭).
5. Idaho.(F.).
6. If I had my way.(F.).
7. Confession.(F.).
8. Shich.(B♭).
9. Shoe China boy.(F.).
10. Honny suckle rose.(F.).
11. Undecided.(F.).
12. China town.(F.).
13. My prayer.(C) of (B♭).
14. The man I love.(E♭).
15. On the sunny side of the street.(B♭).
16. I'm getting sentimental.
17. Georgia.(F.).
18. Alexander ragtime band.(F.).
19. Bye, bye blues.(B♭).
20. After you have gone.(B♭).
21. Blue skys.(F.).
22. Star dust.(E♭).
23. Blue lue.(F.).
24. Darktown strutters ball.(F.).
25. Mood Indigo.(B♭).
26. I'm beginning to see the light.(F.).
27. It had to be you.(F.).
28. Is you is or is you arn't.(F.).
29. The new American petrol.(F.).
30. The flat, fleet floogie.(F.).
31. I may be wrong.(F.).
32. Exactly like you.(B♭).
33. Body and soul.(B♭).
34. My malancholy baby.(F.).

1944

35. I'm gonna love that guy.(B♭).
36. Laughing on the outside.(E♭).
37. Give me five minutes more.(F.).
38. Chickery chick.(F.).
39. Let it snow.(B♭).
40. Dream.(F.).
41. It's a pitty to say good-night.(B♭).
42. Lady be good.(F.).
43. Hé Baberebob.(F.).
44. Take it away.(F.).
45. No can do.(F.).
46. Candy.
47. I can't give you anything but love.(F.).
48. Begin the beguin.(C).
49. You make me love you.
50. Symphonie.(B♭).
51. Get up the stairs.(F.).
52. Shiou, shiou.(F.).
53. Open the door Richard.(F.).
54. A tisket, a tasket.
55. Grootvaders klok.
56. Just a prayer away.(F.).
57. As time goes by.(F.).
58. Little Spanish town.(B).
59. Come out wherever you are.(F.).
60. Accent- schu- ate the possitive.( )
61. 12 Maten blues.
62. In the mood.
63. A little on the lonely side.
64. You fascinating you.
65. Smile.(F.).
66. Shine.(F.).
67. I'll get by.(C.).

Jan Hendriks's Song Chart from the fall of 1944 for his concerts in the Nijmegen concert hall. In his diary, Jan Hendriks mentions additional songs he played for the liberators that are not listed on the song chart, including Farewell Blues, Paper Doll, Tea for Two, I'm in the Mood for Love, Basin Street Blues, and West End Blues.

ories of a time when Dutch citizens had their freedom taken away and fought to regain it. As a personal treasure, Hendriks kept a song chart listing in detail the songs he and his band performed for the liberators in the fall of 1944.

In his concerts, Jan often reminded his audience of the many roles music plays in times of crisis. For him, music was a lifeline, helping him to move forward after enduring terror, destruction, and trauma. 'Looking back', he said, 'for me it was as if I had actually survived the war with music.'

Jan's performances transcended the boundaries of an exclusively Dutch narrative. Between 2015 and 2017, he extended a profoundly generous gesture by inviting me—a German scholar teaching American Studies in the Netherlands—to join him in singing songs that commemorated the joy of regaining freedom. This act of inclusion made me feel humble, grateful, and hopeful.

Jan saw popular music as a powerful force for building bridges across the Atlantic and within Europe. Through music, he connected the past with the present, acknowledged the horrors of war, and delivered a message of hope: music has the power to help us survive and begin the process of healing.[112] Like in the famous scene of the movie *Casablanca* in Rick's Café, I am inclined to say: Play it Again, Jan!

Frank Mehring and pianist Jan Hendriks talk about liberation songs at his last concert shortly before his death at Brebbl in Nijmegen on May 21, 2017.
Photograph: Siax de Bekker

SUITE II: THE SOUNDTRACK OF LIBERATION THEN AND NOW

1 PLAYING LIBERATION SONGS: INTERVIEW WITH JAN HENDRIKS

By Anja Adriaans and Frank Mehring

Jan Hendriks was only fifteen when the Second World War began. His parents owned two shops in the heart of Nijmegen, and the family enjoyed a comfortable, middle-class lifestyle deeply rooted in the city's cultural life. From an early age, the Hendriks children received classical piano lessons at home. Jan, a talented young man, aspired to become an architect. During his high school years, he developed an interest in new and modern styles of music, particularly jazz, which was banned by the German occupiers. Despite the risks, Jan joined several bands, rehearsing at home and performing at private parties. His life became even more turbulent between September 1944 and March 1945, when he started playing in a semi-professional band for the Allied troops who remained stationed in the city and surrounding region. In addition to his musical pursuits, Jan also painted watercolors that accompanied the diary he was writing during this time. Reflecting on that period, he once remarked, 'One minute you're hiding in fear of death from the shells, and the next minute you're entertaining people with music and dance. But perhaps that's what you have to do to survive.'[113]

Jan engaged deeply with his personal experiences of the Second World War by documenting them in a diary. He recorded the events in Nijmegen and his own life from September 1, 1944, to March 18, 1945—the day the last shell fell on Nijmegen, marking the end of its time as a frontline town. With the horrors behind them, the people of Nijmegen could finally begin to rebuild their lives. In 1994, during the 50th anniversary of the war's end, Jan's memories resurfaced so vividly that he quickly painted dozens of watercolors to illustrate the notes in his diary. These artworks, along with his writings, were published in 2004 in his book *Jan Hendriks: Pianist in Bevrijdingstijd, Getekend Dagboek*.

Jan Hendriks went on to become a renowned architect. Even in his later years, he continued to play the piano. He lived with his wife in a house he

Jan Hendriks standing in front of panels for the Nijmegen exhibition The Soundtrack of Liberation with Frank Mehring (l.) and Anja Adriaans (r.) MA students of North American Studies at Radboud University Nijmegen Esther Adema, Litania de Graaf, and Rita Hynes supported the project with their research projects.

designed himself in Mook, near Nijmegen. In the final years of his life, he regularly performed at various locations in and around Nijmegen, commemorating the soundtrack of liberation from 1944 and 1945. Jan passed away on June 10, 2017. This interview was conducted on December 10, 2014, and this book is dedicated to his life and work in the cause of freedom and democracy.

JAN HENDRIKS INTERVIEW

AA: Anja Adriaans, **FM**: Frank Mehring, **JH**: Jan Hendriks

AA: You describe different sorts of performances in your diary. Actually, you began playing at the home of a befriended family during the war, and you played at dance evenings during and after the liberation, but also at official gatherings with military dignitaries?

JH: Yes, that too, on the Kwakkenberg, but it all actually began like this: at the beginning of the war, in 1940, I was a boy of 15 and a pupil at the high school on the Bijleveldsingel. Then in '42, some friends had a gramophone record with jazz by Duke Ellington. I was sold at once and fascinated by this kind music.

We children at home got classical piano lessons from the age of 7. That was something quite different to what it is today, there were studies in scales and broken chords, an awful lot of theory, really dull, no nice songs. But OK, we had to go through with it. Then I came across gramophone records with jazz and I couldn't believe my ears! I fell for it straightaway. My brother was the classical type. He was at grammar school, and he pursued classical music studies and became a concert pianist. Not me—playing the piano was a hobby for me. It wasn't that we were professionals: we listened to it, tried to copy it. Sometimes you had sheet music, but for a long-time sheet music wasn't in the shops.

AA: How did you learn new songs?

JH: Well, we began copying them. In our time, people played all sorts of musical instruments. Guitar, trumpet, saxophone, and, yes, I played the accordion too. There's a photo of me with an accordion in the Valkhof Museum. Things were much homelier in the war years. It wasn't that you couldn't go out, but as a teenager there wasn't a lot to do; you were arrested if it was dark, so you stayed away from public spaces. So, you stayed at home, with friends. Someone would have a new song or an idea, and then someone else. We played at home or at private parties.

AA: You describe the months after the liberation, from September '44, with great intensity in your diary. It was still highly dangerous in Nijmegen and the surrounding area. The time of bombs and shells. A confusing time of freedom and fear. You played a lot at the time. What was it like? How do you recall it?

JH: In October '44, the military leaders of the Allies asked the Dutch military authorities to organize social activities for the troops stationed here, dance evenings for example. That was a problem in Catholic Nijmegen! A plan was needed. An organization was set up, the Twenty-One Club.[114] The Dutch military authorities had to organize something quickly because otherwise the situation would get out of hand.

AA: Can you tell us a little more about it?

JH: At the end of October there were 100,000 Allied personnel here, but at the end of November it had become 200,000, and at the end of January already 400,000, all that on top of a population of 100,000, 20,000 of whom had fled the city. So something had to be done.

The Twenty-One Club was set up as controlled diversion for the soldiers. It had little to do with liberation celebrations. Adult girls from 'good homes' could register. Well, it really took off, but it worked for only 48 hours, and then it was every man for himself. The Church couldn't stop it; after all, we had been liberated by these soldiers. So it all went ahead anyway. The idea for a club was a complete failure, although it carried on for a while. In concert hall 'de Vereeniging' there was a band which played once a week, Saturdays, but it spread further because everywhere else there were dance evenings and parties going on. In schools, factory canteens and in big villas that had been commandeered, and on the Westerhelling, I played there too.

AA: And you played there with your band too after the liberation, so from September '44 onward?

JH: Yes, one of us—not me—they did the organizing, and they knew the army officers, dates were passed on, 'Can you play here or there tonight?', and then you were picked up, mostly by a truck. Every evening, I played a different piano or even a grand piano. The other band members brought their own instruments with them, but I just had to keep getting used to the pianos.

I was the youngest and an amateur and Jack Doorman, the drummer, was also an amateur. The others were lads who had arrived following the troops to Nijmegen. They were from Amsterdam, and they were professionals. The gigs in the war. They might well have played for the Germans too, but they never said so. But OK, they had played in Eindhoven and Maastricht, and they wanted to go back, but they got no further. They weren't allowed to go to the north of the Netherlands.

'Swingtime for our liberators, Nov. 5, 1944.' Watercolor by Jan Hendriks, 2004. Jan Hendriks Collection

At the beginning, I didn't know anybody in the group. The first performance with this band was at a villa in Malden, I still don't know where it was. It was really nice. The owners weren't there. Maybe they had fled, I don't know. There was no money. We were to ask 32 guilders per person and it was paid in kind, cigarettes and canned food. My family, of course, were delighted. On many evenings there was an awful lot of drink, always spirits, whisky, and rum. I didn't drink that. Sometimes I brought an empty bottle and funnel with me and negotiated the drink later. That was trading in those times.

FM: When and how did the feeling of liberation influence the music? Was that in September '44 or later?

JH: During the early days of the liberation in September '44, nobody actually knew precisely what was happening. Later, when the Allied troops stayed here, sometimes for months on end, there was a special atmosphere. Well, the soldiers, they had time to spare, they were boys of 18, 24 years of age, they could rest here. The streets were full of jeeps, trucks, tanks, they liked the girls of course, there were plenty of them on the streets. People in Nijmegen invited them into their homes.

FM: What does liberation music mean to you?

JH: It is a deep feeling that you can do whatever you want. If I play the note so and so, as long as it's within the rules of the chord, then I'll do it, and no one is going to tell me any different. You can like it or hate it, but I couldn't care less. And playing together, you communicate with each other in the music, I had great fun making music. But I do write in my diary that it can be tedious too.

Sometimes you had the situation at the same location that one evening was terrific and another was nothing, because the soldiers were getting bored or were half drunk. We always knew when they were being sent to the front the next day, because then they got extra drink. Well, the war was still going on after all. There was still a great deal of fighting. Yes, you know, the soldiers... they didn't know, 'Will I still be alive tomorrow or not?' They took it as it came.

AA: What tunes did you play on those evenings?

JH: I don't know whether it'll do you any good, but I managed to find this, the original list of the tunes we played. They're all American or English tunes that we played with the band. That is what we played on the dance evenings for the Allies. There were different evenings: you had what you'd call soft evenings and you had swing evenings.

AA: This list was assembled in 1944. Did you already know all these tunes at the time? And you didn't have sheet music?

JH: Yes, we often knew the songs. At that time, you could buy nothing, absolutely nothing. Only at the beginning of the war, in 1940-1941, you could still go to a shop and get something from under the counter. And we listened to the English radio. English and American music was banned; you weren't allowed to have it and you weren't allowed to play it. But we knew it. In 1933 we had already heard American bands, Louis Armstrong, and Duke Ellington; he came to the Netherlands and played here.

If you read about it in the papers back then, it was unbelievable. They wrote, 'what dreadful music', 'hip-swinging music', 'sexual histrionics, it should all be banned'. Public opinion considered it indecent and inappropriate music.

This was an unknown, unfamiliar culture that had come to the Netherlands. At the time, the Netherlands was an ultraconservative country, unbelievable if you compare it with today. It was a kind of religious dictatorship, totally no freedom, enormous social control. Every Sunday we went to church. The slightest thing meant you were committing a deadly sin.

In that context the free music came into our homes and that had nothing to do with religion, and because it was at home and at parties and birthdays, we could practice and play it, freely.

AA: So you also played jazz?

JH: The Dutch population was opposed to the Germans, no question about that. There was only one thing they agreed on: jazz was abominable music. My father and mother said: 'My God, what on earth are you up to? What awful music.' But they were OK with me coming home with the band and creating a cacophony. That was really good of them, but they wanted nothing to do with it themselves. The music was not appreciated. But then the group I'm talking about, that time of dance and liberation, I was that age, I was in the thick of it, we were the boys and girls of the time, the girls even more than the boys. The little bands we had at the time—that was not yet the Liberation Band, I only got to know them later—, the improvising, the music gave you such a feeling of freedom. It was indescribable, really strange. But it passed again when the soldiers left; it was a short, intense period. So jazz existed earlier, but it was called 'nigger music'.

FM: Is that a term that the Dutch used too, that name?

JH: Yes, really true. Everyone called it 'negroid music'. Even in the papers: if you read newspapers from the thirties about the bands that came here, you'll be astonished. If we were to read that sort of thing today. Discrimination, that word was invented later, in my youth the word didn't exist; people just said 'darky' or 'nigger' if you were dark-skinned. (...)

AA: Were there any special songs that have stayed with you? Songs that belonged to the time of the war?

Jan Hendriks as a young man at the end of WWII

JH: Songs that were known in the war, songs from the war: *Als Sterren Flonkerend aan de Hemel Staan*, *Een zonnig Madeira*, *Dag Schatteboutje*, Ouwe *Taaie*; Jackie (Jack) Bulterman was well-known. He wrote happy songs, he was a member of The Ramblers. He sang and composed and arranged too. Bulterman and The Ramblers played at 'de Vereeniging', once or twice a year.

AA: But you played there sometimes too, with the band?

JH: Yes, but that was only after the liberation. They had collaborated in fact, they were cleared by the Dutch Kulturkammer (Chamber of Culture during the war) because they had registered and joined, they were punished for that later too; they weren't allowed to perform in the Netherlands for six months after the war. They went straight to Belgium and played in Antwerp and Brussels every night, and then they came back here.

FM: There is a song called *Ik kan niet swingen*; it means, 'I want to but I don't know how'. Did you know the song in 1945, did you play that too?

JH: I don't know that song. In the war you didn't hear or play swing. Afterwards yes, it all went so fast. The music and the war, for me the music and the war were one. *The Hokey Pokey* yes, I do know that. We played it every night. Then we simply made it stop. The girls learned it quickly. Then they made circles and danced it, even on the street. It was actually English, not American. *Under the Chestnut Tree* was another really popular English dance.

JH: There are two things that I just want to emphasize. So, there was swing. And afterwards, the Americans, who joined up voluntarily, and the Canadians at the beginning, came here to Europe, leaving their families behind. That was often out of poverty, so the blacks joined up, they were truck personnel or kitchen personnel, they had to polish boots. We know so much now, but we knew so little then. (...) Those boys left their country, often for years on end. And fantastic songs were made about that by composers in America, Cole Porter for example and others. But they were melancholic songs. *I'll be seeing you*, *Sentimental Journey*... We played two sorts in fact, the swing alternating with the soft, somehow melancholic, songs, *I'll Get By* and *As Time Goes By*. We played those too.

AA: Were there also songs that belonged especially to the time directly after the war? We mentioned earlier that there was little time to experience your grief or to remember the dead. After the liberation, people quickly turned to rebuilding.

JH: For example, there was the song *Als op het Leidseplein de lichtjes weer eens branden gaan*, which is a famous postwar song and, of course, *Eens zal de Betuwe weer in bloei staan*. That was just after the war, because the Betuwe had been laid waste. That was a transition that was quickly over after 1950. You must realize, people wanted to move on as quickly as possible. There must have been more, but even I don't know them all. And others were nine-day wonders. That is still the case today.

The Chestnut Tree, cover (1939)

FM: There was a lot of music that was never recorded. *Trees heeft een Canadees*, everyone knows it. That song was recorded several times. But there were lots more along the same lines: *Mijn Tommy uit Canada*, *Mamma, zijn naam is Johnny*, *Little Holland Girl*, *Groeten aan Amerika*—those are songs that also deal with girls and Allied soldiers, but they weren't recorded.

AA: Was there a generally accepted form of music before that time? You talk about music not being appreciated, which was indecent or unheard of, or sounded like nothing, but what was liked?

Little Holland Girl, back (1945)

JH: You had folk songs, Lou Bandy, *Daar bij die Molen*, *Van je hela hola*, and there was lots of marching music. A great deal from Sousa,[115] also an American. You had the KLM March. Here in Nijmegen we had lots of shoe factories, the Robinson, Swift, they all had their own bands or choirs. And the lads at the slaughterhouse had all kinds of songs of their own, which they sang and whistled. You had the Air Force Band, the Navy Band, that's all marching music. They also played to make propaganda with other music mixed in, but it was the marching music which stayed. There were some new ones in it, but they then always reverted to the original marching music.

FM: Is that liberation music too?

JH: Actually, it has little to do with liberation, I think. For instance, you also have a Four Days March, so there are lots of songs that are not directly related to the war and liberation.

FM: Maybe with patriotism though. The homeland, the beloved Netherlands.

JH: It was a weird and dangerous time. How did I survive it? The really crazy thing is that you're right there in the thick of it. I read about it again now and think how it was seventy years ago. I could have been dead too. But you know, you can't hang around in the cellar all day and, yes, [in Nijmegen] eight hundred people didn't survive it and many were wounded. But people adapt quickly, don't they? And my father didn't say: listen, you're not going out to play tonight, OK?

Looking back, for me it was as if I had actually survived the war with music.

2
EXHIBITING LIBERATION SONGS: THE FREEDOM MUSEUM

Rense Havinga

Music is a universal constant throughout history. It's hard to think of a single time and place where people did not express their feelings through songs and use music as a means of entertainment and escape. During the Second World War, music was employed as a tool of propaganda by both the Axis powers and the Allies, by the occupiers and the resistance members. Music was composed and performed on battlefields, in hiding places, and in concentration camps. At times, music was even used as a cruel weapon, such as when Jewish musicians were forced to perform in concentration camps before and during executions.

One might expect historians to utilize music as a valuable resource. Like diaries and interviews, music provides insight into the emotions and experiences of those who lived through historical events. Sadly, however, music is often overlooked as a source of information and as a tool in historical exhibitions. Historians conducting research consult paper archives far more frequently than audio databanks, and historic literature rarely includes a soundtrack of the times. The audio components in exhibitions are often chosen long after the texts have been written, rendering it inconsequential if a 60s jazz tune plays over liberation footage from the 1940s. This represents a significant missed opportunity, as songs can offer valuable information—not just about the history of music itself, but about virtually any historical topic.

Welcome Boy, cover (1945)

To illustrate this, let me take you through the history of Allied soldiers and their relationships with Dutch women. Music related to this topic came to my attention while working on the exhibition *Canadian War Brides: A One-Way Passage to Love*, which was on display at the Freedom Museum in Groesbeek in 2012.[116] Most of these songs can be found in the Keesing Collection, donated to the museum by Hugo Keesing that same year.

The first Allied soldiers arrived in the Netherlands in September 1944. Much of southern Netherlands was liberated in the fall of 1944, and many Allied soldiers spent the winter there, moving in with the locals. After the Battle of the Rhineland in early 1945, the northeast of the Netherlands was liberated in April 1945. The major cities in the west were liberated only when the occupying forces surrendered on May 5th. In the days that followed, Canadian forces entered the major cities of Holland as triumphant heroes. As it turned out, the Canadians in particular were there to stay: the war in the Pacific was still ongoing, and no ships were available to transport all these soldiers back home. About 170,000 Canadian soldiers remained in the Netherlands until after August 1945, with over half not being repatriated until January 1946. The Canadians settled in, got to know the locals, and developed a particular fondness for Dutch women. For over 18 months, the presence of Allied soldiers was a part of Dutch life.

In the euphoria of liberation, it briefly seemed like anything was possible. The gratitude towards the Allied soldiers was immense, with girls vying to be the first to kiss a soldier and parents turning a blind eye to many of these intimate encounters. After all, the liberators deserved some reward for their efforts, and hadn't attention from women always been the reward for military heroes? In the imagery of the time, the Netherlands itself is often depicted as a woman embracing her male liberators. Within this context, a Dutch girl dancing with an Allied soldier was simply performing her duty on behalf of a grateful nation. In this atmosphere, there was an abundance of love songs.

MIJN TOMMY UIT CANADA

Omdat ik mijn Tommy heb ben ik zo blij
Trots loop ik door de stad, Tom aan m'n zij
Vol van vreugde kijkt ons nu een ieder na
Mijn wens is thans vervuld
Hij neemt mij later mee naar Canada

MY TOMMY FROM CANADA

I'm so pleased now that I have my Tommy
Walking proudly through the city, Tom at my side
Everyone is filled with joy as they look at us
My wish has been fulfilled.
He'll take me home to Canada.

MAMMA, ZIJN NAAM IS JOHNNY

Mamma, zijn naam is Johnny, de Tommy waar ik van hou.
Mamma, hij's mijn bon-bon-nie, 'k denk dat ik hem trouw.
'k heb nu mijn keus gevonden, ik huur straks een huis in Londen.
Altijd met hem verbonden, Mamma, I'm happy now.

Mijn Tommy uit Canada, cover (1945)

MAMMA, HIS NAME IS JOHNNY

Mamma, his name is Johnny, the Tommy that I love.
Mamma, he's my sweetheart, I think I'll marry him.
I have found my choice now, I'll rent a house in London.
Always with him united, Mamma, I'm happy now.

Mamma, zijn naam is Johnny, cover (1945)

But as the joy of liberation wore off, the romance lost some of its appeal. In the months that followed, the Canadians who remained became less heroic in the eyes of the Dutch. Many people complained that the Canadians were occupying houses that belonged to the Dutch and trading on the black market. In a country in dire need of currency reform, cigarettes became the most reliable form of currency, and Canadian soldiers had an ample supply. Soldiers with nothing but time on their hands became unruly and got into fights after a night out. Among the problems of having 170,000 soldiers around, the most controversial was the spread of sexually transmitted diseases and the rising number of single mothers resulting from relationships between Canadian soldiers and Dutch girls. Estimates of the number of illegitimate children born to the girlfriends of allied soldiers in the Netherlands range from 5,000 to 8,000. In a country where single mothers were still considered highly problematic, this caused great distress. A popular joke about the number of illegitimate children in the postwar period ran: 'If another war starts in 20 years, the Canadians won't need to send an army; a ship full of uniforms will suffice.' On top of all that, Dutch men were jealous of the young heroes in uniform.

When popular opinion turned against the soldiers, none were more affected than the girls and women who dated them. After all, the Dutch owed the Canadian soldiers some gratitude, but they did not owe the girls anything. Popular opinion turned against them with a vengeance, and the songs published later in 1945 reflect this, ranging from stern warnings to accusations.

DAG SJAAN, DAG BEP, DAG ALIDA

Sjaantje's Tom heeft bioscopen
Beppie's Bill is miljonair
Ali's John heeft zelfs een vliegtuig
Want hij is een Broadway-ster
't is te hopen lieve kinderen,
Dat dit waarheid is gewis
En je man geen putjesschepper
Of een kidnap-gangster is
Anders zit je in de kou
Met dit dollar-prins van jou.

BYE SJAAN, BYE BEP, BYE ALIDA

Sjaantje's Tom has cinemas
Beppie's Bill is a millionaire
Ali's John has his own airplane
For he's a Broadway star
I do hope, my dear children
That all of this is true
And your husband is no
sewage worker or kidnap gangster
Otherwise you'll be in the cold
With your dollar prince

DE CANADEESCHE KOORTS

Mijn vrouw heeft Canadeesche koorts
Ze is niet te genezen
Ze danst, drinkt cocktails enzoovoort
Alleen met Canadeezen
Haar Engelsch is niet al te best
'T is Yes en No en voor de rest
Doet zij het met gebarenspel
Van *kusgeluid* u weet het wel
Een hand een zoentje enzoovoorts
De Canadeesche koorts

Mijn vrouw moet blijkbaar dag en nacht
De Canadeezen bijstaan
En ik moet daarom uren lang
Voor eten in de rij staan
Mijn huisgezin loopt in de war
Omdat m'n vrouw geen tijd heeft
Zij viert maar feest en doet precies
Of zij ons land bevrijd heeft

THE CANADIAN FEVER

My wife has the Canadian fever
She cannot be cured

Dag Sjaan, Dag Bep, Dag Alida, cover (1945)

She dances, drinks cocktails and so on
Only with Canadians
Her English isn't good
It's yes and no and for the rest
She uses sign language

And *kissing noises*, well you know
A hand, a kiss, and so on
The Canadian fever

My wife needs to go out day and night
To support the Canadians
And I need to spend hours a day
Standing in line for food
My family is in mayhem
Because my wife doesn't have time
She's out partying and acting as if
She liberated our country.

By the end of 1945, the mood had soured in some places, with reports emerging of Dutch men harassing the girlfriends of Canadian soldiers. These men threatened to shave the women's heads—a punishment previously inflicted by the Dutch on girls who had dated German soldiers. Criticism of Dutch girls began to take on a nationalist tone, with accusations that they were traitors to their country for choosing a non-Dutch partner.

MEISJE, LET OP JE ZAAK

Neerlandsch meisje, was je vroeger
Om je netheid steeds bekend
Ga zoo door, dan maak je spoedig
Aan je goede naam 'n end
Velen die met Moffen heulden
Hebben daarvoor reeds gebrand
Meisje, ook gij zijt verraadster
Van de eer van Nederland
Menschen kwamen en zij gingen
Ook de Tommy gaat weer heen
Denk dan niet dat hij je meeneemt
Meisje, dan sta je weer alleen

De Canadeesche Koorts, cover (1945)

Hollandsch Meisje, cover (1945)

GIRL, WATCH WHAT YOU DO

Dutch girl, you used to be
Known for your good intent
Keep this up and soon
That good name will end.
Many who collaborated with the Germans
Have already burned for it
You too are a traitor
To the honor of the Dutch
People have come and gone
The Tommies too will go
Don't think they will take you home
Girl, you'll be on your own again.

When the last Allied soldiers left the Netherlands in the spring of 1946, the debate lost its venom, and the Dutch public soon forgot about their own harsh treatment of the girls. The only ones who continued to suffer the scorn of society were the many single mothers raising children in the postwar period. Public memories of the Allied soldiers became more positive, and while memories of the perceived immorality of Dutch girls persisted, they were now surrounded by an air of nostalgia and romance. Of the many songs written about these relationships, only the highly popular song *Trees heeft een Canadees* endured in public memory. It offers a few firm words of advice to the Dutch girls but maintains an overall positive tone. Songs like *Girl, Watch What You Do* and *The Canadian Fever* lost their appeal to an audience eager to romanticize the history of liberation.

The story of Allied soldiers and Dutch girls is just one example of how changing societal attitudes are reflected in the songs of the time. There are many such songs on various topics, providing valuable source material and an excellent medium for sharing these stories with a broader audience. The song lyrics are often simple, accessible to many, and carry both emotion and information, conveying the sentiments of that period to an audience that may struggle to imagine what it was truly like to live in 1945.

Music, as has been true through the centuries, continues to entertain. While this may seem insignificant from an academic perspective, it is vital for a museum. Many historical stories will be read by few and remembered

Vredesmarsch, cover (1945)

by even fewer if we cannot capture the audience's attention, surprise them with new information, and leave them feeling both educated and entertained.

CODA

Frank Mehring

The Freedom Museum in Groesbeek deploys a rich array of historical sources, including songs, photographs, and other memorabilia, to craft an emotional and immersive connection to the past. Central to this narrative is the recognition of the pivotal role played by Allied forces during the liberation of the Netherlands in World War II. The museum's special exhibition, *Love in Wartime* (June 5, 2024—March 30, 2025), exemplifies this approach by using artifacts such as sheet music and photographs to explore the profound relationship between love and war. The exhibition illustrates that, throughout history, love has been inextricably linked to periods of conflict, with the omnipresence of death often heightening the yearning for life and intimacy. This dynamic was especially pronounced during World War II, when the war shaped the romantic experiences of an entire generation.

The exhibition offers a deeply personal view of war and liberation, revealing the intimate, human side of the conflict through love stories that often had far-reaching consequences. One significant outcome was the migration of thousands of war brides to and from the Netherlands, which profoundly affected both the women who left their homes and the men they married. The children born to both Allied and German soldiers during the war further complicate the legacies left by these relationships, leaving cultural and familial imprints that extended long after the war's end.[117] Through these stories, *Love in Wartime* highlights the ways in which love persisted and evolved amidst the chaos of conflict.

One of the exhibition's most evocative displays is a showcase featuring an invitation from Canadian soldiers to a dance party for Dutch women: 'The Canadian Unit will have a dance party next Friday, the 17th of November 1944, from 7 until 11 o'clock at Boarding House Marienbosch, Groesbeek-Scheweg. The ladies of this city are cordially invited; you are all welcome to join. Starts at 7 o'clock, ends at 11 o'clock.'[118] This seemingly lighthearted invitation underscores the complex social dynamics of the time, as young Dutch men began to feel marginalized, struggling to compete with the elevated status of the Allied liberators. As the initial euphoria of liberation faded, tensions grew between the Dutch population and the Canadian soldiers who remained in the country, with some Dutch citizens complaining about the soldiers occupying homes and engaging in black market activities.

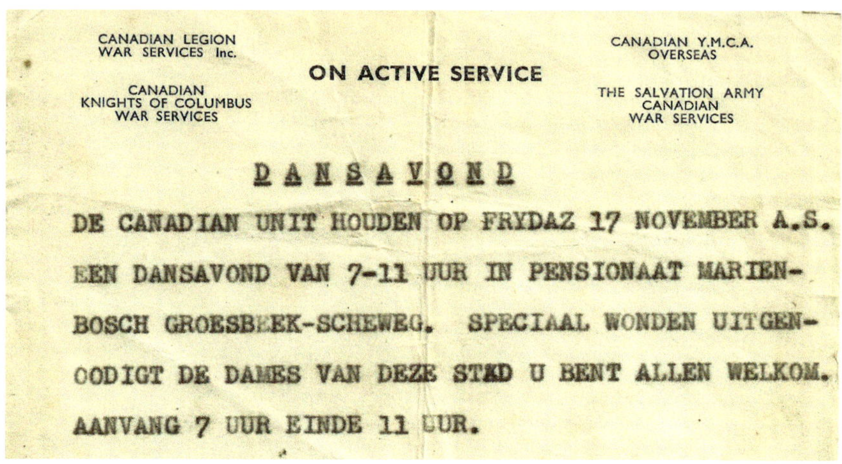

CANADIAN LEGION
WAR SERVICES Inc.

CANADIAN
KNIGHTS OF COLUMBUS
WAR SERVICES

ON ACTIVE SERVICE

CANADIAN Y.M.C.A.
OVERSEAS

THE SALVATION ARMY
CANADIAN
WAR SERVICES

DANSAVOND

DE CANADIAN UNIT HOUDEN OP FRYDAZ 17 NOVEMBER A.S.
EEN DANSAVOND VAN 7-11 UUR IN PENSIONAAT MARIEN-
BOSCH GROESBEEK-SCHEWEG. SPECIAAL WONDEN UITGEN-
OODIGT DE DAMES VAN DEZE STAD U BENT ALLEN WELKOM.
AANVANG 7 UUR EINDE 11 UUR.

Invitation by Canadian soldiers to a dance for Dutch girls. © Freedom Museum

The exhibition further deepens its emotional impact through the display of a piano adorned with two glasses of champagne, symbolizing the festive, yet fleeting, nature of wartime celebrations. Alongside the piano is sheet music for songs like *Mijn Tommy uit Canada* and *Trees heeft een Canadees,* which visitors can explore digitally, gaining access to both the scores and lyrics. The inclusion of these songs serves as a poignant reminder of the cultural exchanges that took place during the war, as well as the emotional resonance that music can provide in times of uncertainty and loss. Notably, the collection of sheet music and postcards, donated by Hugo Keesing, is woven into the museum's narrative, providing a sense of closure as Keesing's personal engagement with the material finds its place in the ongoing dialog about memory, history, and love during wartime.

By presenting war and liberation through the lens of personal experience, *Love in Wartime* offers visitors a unique opportunity to engage with

Hugo Keesing at the Freedom Museum, Sep. 12, 2024. © F. Mehring

the most intimate aspects of human life during one of history's most tumultuous periods. The exhibition not only sheds light on the complexities of romantic relationships during war, but also invites reflection on the lasting legacies of these stories, emphasizing that even in the darkest times, love endures, adapts, and transforms.

Happy people on Liberation Day in Hertogplein in front of the *Nutsschool*, far left Derde Walstraat. Regionaal Archief Nijmegen

A billeted Allied soldier has her picture taken with daughter Ida of H. Speijers Bakery. Sep. 1944. Regionaal Archief Nijmegen. Photographic Archive Anna Huybers

3
COLLECTING LIBERATION SONGS: A TRANSATLANTIC QUEST

Hugo A. Keesing

FACT: Well over 350 pieces of sheet music dealing with Holland and World War II were published between 1938 and 1948. It is quite possible that fewer than 50 were formally recorded. Approximately 30 titles dealt with the prewar mobilization period. About twice that number dealt with aspects of the occupation. Some 160 titles can be termed liberation songs and another 40 focused on the postwar reconstruction period.

FACT: For more than 60 years, despite the resources and holdings of numerous war-related museums, archives and other repositories, there had been no comprehensive, institutional attempt to identify, locate, catalog and preserve this part of Holland's history.

FACT: In 2012, the donation of a private collection, assembled by an American born in The Hague during the war, returned much of that music to its rightful home. Here is the story about who, what, how and why the soundtrack of Holland's war years first came about and then came home.

Perhaps it was in The Hague, March 3, 1945. On that day, the RAF accidently dropped their bombs on the Bezuidenhout neighborhood instead of the German V2 installation in the Haagse Bos. One of those bombs leveled Adelheidstraat 145 where the Keesing family had just moved their belongings after another errant bomb had damaged their home a few blocks away. On that day, virtually every belonging, including my father's book and stamp collections, disappeared. Saving our history, be it photos, letters or 'things', took on added importance and led every family member except my mother to become collectors. Her task was to refrain from disposing of the collections, even as we went away to school or moved into our own homes.

Perhaps the reason has roots in the Keesing family tree. One branch began the Keesing Historisch Archief in 1911. As part of Systemen Keesing it was an early effort to collect, analyze, evaluate, and publish financial and other data. My own branch of the tree includes Opa Keesing, a collector of anecdotes and drawings that caught his interest, whose sense of humor is accurately captured in the well-known diary of Anne Frank. Opa was 'the old fogey who teaches math', and assigned her extra work as punishment for talking too much in class. I can add that my father was a professor on the Economics faculty at the University of Amsterdam and my mother was one of Holland's first teachers trained by Maria Montessori in her educational methods.

Another possible reason has to do with being uprooted in 1951, at age 7, from a Dutch postwar setting still showing many of the scars of five years of occupation to the relative tranquility of Washington, DC. The United States was about to begin eight years with the former Supreme Commander, Allied Expeditionary Forces, General Dwight D. Eisenhower, as its President. Equally if not more important, the decade of the 1950s would place a spotlight on youths that in turn would create a youth-oriented pop-

Record Label, The Platters: *The Great Pretender* (1957). Photograph by Hugo Keesing ular culture in media that included music. Familiarity with the 'new' music of rock 'n' roll was one way in which a boy born and raised in Holland could assimilate into the peer culture of his American classmates.

In some combination, these and other antecedents turned me first into a collector, then a student and finally a teacher of popular culture. The collecting began with postcards, gum cards, comic books and phonograph records. Even as the family moved from home to home, none of the collections were lost or thrown away. Having once lost almost everything, the family philosophy was 'hold on to it, you never know when you may use/need it someday.' That held especially true for my 45-rpm record collection that was begun in 1955.

Beginning with my first purchase, the Platters' *The Great Pretender*, my genetic predisposition kicked in. I assigned the record #1 and noted both the A and B sides on a piece of lined paper. And so the cataloging started. By 1957, I had collected almost 100 records that were stored in two carrying cases, behind tabs that made their retrieval simple. I took them to parties where I became the *de facto* disc jockey, a role that demanded that I also be knowledgeable of the artist, the record label and related minutiae. Possibly this early career path also discouraged me from ever learning to read music or play an instrument.

Record collecting remained my primary hobby through college and graduate school. By the time I finished my graduate work in the field of Behavior Research/Psychology and was ready to begin my doctoral research, I owned some 1500 records, cross-indexed by artist and title, all in white sleeves that indicated their place in my collection as well as the date that they entered and their highest position on the U.S. 'Hot 100 Charts'. I had also begun purchasing music books. In 1969, with Carl Belz's *The Story of Rock*, Nik Cohn's *Rock From the Beginning* and Jonathan Eisen's (Ed.) *The Age of Rock*, writings on pop music took on a new approach. Where previously writing superficial paperbacks for the fans of Elvis Presley and the Beatles, the new wave of writers placed music and its audience in a broader cultural context, along the lines of Bob Dylan's *The Times They Are a-Changin'*. Through my collecting I had unconsciously begun assembling the resources that would result in *Youth in Transition: A Content Analysis of Two Decades of Popular Music*, one of the earliest dissertations on the music of the 1950s and 1960s, to fulfill the requirements for a PhD.

Because my research required accurate lyrics, and transcribing songs based on what I 'heard' on records was neither easy nor reliable, I began purchasing sheet music for songs in my data sample. So started yet another collection.

By the early 1970s, I had earned my doctorate and was teaching psychology courses to U.S. military students stationed in Europe and Asia. Many of those students had grown up with the music of the previous two decades so they responded well when I interjected musical examples to illustrate psychological concepts. This proved especially true in courses such as social psychology and adolescent psychology. It wasn't long before I developed a course plan that would focus on music and other examples of pop culture with both psychological and historical underpinnings. In 1976, the University of Maryland approved it as a special topics course in the American Studies department.

From humble beginnings with 18–25 students, the course quickly grew in popularity. By the mid-1980s, enrollments were capped at 300 students. Entitled 'Popular Music in American Society', classes traced recent history from 1940 forward. The first class moved quickly from the Big Band Era to World War II. Subsequent classes addressed the Cold War, Elvis, civil rights, the space race, the war in Vietnam and dozens of other topics and events that shaped America's history.

Because popular music had the information sharing role of today's social media, it quickly responded to newsworthy events. For example, songs about the killing of four students at Kent State University (1970), the Watergate scandal that forced President Nixon's resignation (1974), natural events like the eruption of Mount St. Helens (1980) and 'firsts' such as astronaut Sally Ride's journey into space (1983) came into the collection. Thanks to song writers I had a constant stream of new, topical material with which to work.

While my initial sheet music purchases were pop songs, I soon became interested in World War II era songs. First, because they said so much about the country's home front response and second, because I could find very little academic research on the topic. When I had acquired about 600 war-related sheets, I thought it time to do a 'comprehensive' listing/cataloging of the collection. Just to be on the safe side I decided I needed to do a quick check at the Library of Congress to see if I was missing a substan-

Ons Holland is vrij, cover (1945)

tial number of songs. Fifteen weeks and thousands of titles later I knew I had uncovered only the proverbial tip of the iceberg. Serious collecting of World War II songs began about 30 years ago.

It was in the Netherlands, visiting my mother, that a Dutch subset of the collection came into being. I had located several stores, Muziekbeurs

Amsterdam, Broekmans & Van Poppel, and others, that had large amounts of 'oude bladmuziek'. In systematically going through their stock, I found numerous examples that by their cover art and/or title, for example *Ons Holland is vrij,* were clearly war-related. So, I bought them, generally for a euro or less, and took them back home with me to add to the overall collection. There they sat next to a small number of Dutch-themed U.S. sheets with titles like *The Old Dutch Mill Will Turn Again* and *The Tulips Are Talking Tonight.*

When my mother passed away in 1993, I found six postcards among the papers she had saved. They were drawn by Pax Steen and proved to be part of a 1945 series 'Vrij Holland viert feest!' (Free Netherlands is celebrating). That she had held on to them for almost 50 years caused me to reevaluate what these mementos of the liberation had meant to her. It also aroused my curiosity as to whether there had been more music and more cards like these. The answer to both, of course, was 'Yes'. A year later Joop van Houten's *Nederland bevrijd: een muzikale terugblik op de meidagen van '45* (Reba, 1994) paired the two popular expressions of the liberation in an illustrated book. Its images fueled my desire to locate and acquire the 'original' objects. I also came across two paperbacks by Co de Kloet (*Morgen komt een nieuwe dag: Liedjes van en om de oorlog;* Fontein, 1990 and *Trees heeft een Canadees: De bekendste liedjes rondom de bevrijding*; Fontein, 1995) that prompted me to focus on the Dutch sheets as a separate collection.

As I began my search for more sheets and cards, I turned to the internet, specifically eBay.nl and Marktplaats.nl. Browsing categories connected to 'bevrijding 1945' not only helped me locate them, it also introduced me to books, pamphlets, postage stamps, plates, plaques, puzzles, posters, and more. It started me reading about the post-1945 period that I was too young to remember. The more I read, the more determined I became to learn all I could from my two primary sources.

On subsequent trips to Holland, I visited such places as the Royal Library of the Netherlands (*Koninklijke Bibliotheek*), the NIOD Institute for War, Holocaust and Genocide Studies, *Theater Instituut Nederland*, the Resistance Museum (*Verzetsmuseum*), and the Freedom Museum to determine their holdings and to refine my growing databases in both areas.

Vrij Holland viert feest postcards (1945)

What I learned was that none of the institutions had specific, significant collections of either. A few music sheets, some incomplete series or random cards, none with any sign of scholarship to place them in context, were all I could find. It was at that point that I told myself the collections, at the point where I believed I had taken them as far as I could, would have to be returned to Holland.

In 2012, I approached the Liberation Museum by way of email and was fortunate to receive a response a day later from Curator Rense Havinga. I asked about its current liberation sheet music holdings—five pieces—and inquired about the museum's ability and willingness to catalog, digitize, and provide proper care and safekeeping for the music. As an educator I also asked what the museum might do to provide research access to the collection. In ensuing exchanges, he assured me of the former and said that 'very good contacts with the Radboud University Nijmegen' left him confident that someone qualified would come to look at the materials. Based on Rense's assurances

I carried more than 300 pieces across the Atlantic in a backpack and placed them in his care. Many of the pieces in this book and in the exhibit produced by the Liberation Museum in 2015 came out of that backpack.

Holland, cover (1945)

In 2013, after the pieces were cataloged in the museum archive and high resolution scans had been made of all their pages, they were reintroduced to their homeland. Rense regularly informed me, in writing and with photos, when one or more pieces found their way into the museum's rotating exhibits such as *Canadian War Brides* and *From Drees to Frank Sinatra: The period of rebuilding after WW2.* He also told me that someone from the American Studies department at the Radboud University had become interested in the collection. That someone was Frank Mehring.

A year later, I learned the full extent of Frank's interest in the music, particularly the liberation songs. Among other things they bring to life the silent images of unbounded joy, relief and national pride felt in those May days. They also give voice to the spontaneous interactions between liberators and those who were liberated. For example, several songs address the cultural divides created by different languages—Dutch and English—and styles of music and dance like 'rhythm' and 'swing'. In short, the sheets have made it possible to recreate an actual soundtrack of the liberation with Dutch songs rather than the more familiar but imported songs of Glenn Miller, The Andrews Sisters, or Vera Lynn. Frank's work has added both meaning and value to what previously had been colorful, provocative cover images and words written over music symbols (notes) that had no meaning for me. In his hands, they were transformed into living, breathing songs and dances. I cannot adequately describe what it was like to sit in the front row for the first two performances of the 'Soundtrack of Liberation' in September 2014 except to say that it brought tears to my eyes.

As the collaboration between the museum and the university continues, I am absolutely convinced that parting with my collection and bringing the music home was the right thing to do. This book and the exhibit further reinforce my long-standing belief in the power of music to inform, to entertain, and to educate. I hope it is doing so for you as well.

4
COMPOSING LIBERATION MUSIC: A SYMPHONY

Dean Burry

Given the desire of the arts to reflect and comment on the human experience, it is unsurprising that so many artists—painters, writers, and musicians—have been inspired by war. One could argue that the strengths and weaknesses of the human race are never more apparent than in times of extreme duress. The Second World War served as a brutally honest mirror of who we are, and countless artists over the last century have seized upon the topic as a sort of dark muse—the destruction of war starkly contrasting with the creation of art.

The songs of liberation and the music of wartime undoubtedly resonate far beyond the periods in which they were first heard. Every country had its own soundtrack: to mourn during tragic times, to raise spirits during challenges, to celebrate in moments of triumph, and to reflect on the aftermath once the shooting had ceased. As a young boy growing up in the former British colony of Canada during the seventies, I remember learning the music of England's war experience in school: the songs of Vera Lynn and the big band music of the Americans, Tommy Dorsey, and Glenn Miller. Music has a unique way of embedding itself in a person's subconscious, and decades later those soundtracks—now enriched by the songs of France, Italy, and the Netherlands—have blossomed into the inspiration for something larger.

After two decades working as a freelance composer, I received an appointment to the DAN School of Drama and Music at Queen's University in Kingston, Ontario. Teaching wasn't new to me, but I had only dipped my toe in the pool of higher-level academic research. As a composer (with admittedly varied musical tastes), I generally didn't write papers but rather operas, musicals, symphonies, and folk songs (I grew up on the island of Newfoundland and never abandoned my love of sea shanties). So when the university offered me a research initiation grant, I wasn't quite sure what to make of it. After reassurance from my colleagues that research-creation was indeed encouraged, I landed on a topic I had stumbled across twenty years earlier and filed away in the back of my mind: the Canadian war artist. A quick trip to the library revealed the book *Alex Colville: Diary of a War Artist*, compiled by Graham Metson and Cheryl Lean. What immediately struck me was that the iconic Canadian painter Alex Colville and I attended the same undergraduate school, Mount Allison University on the East Coast, albeit fifty-two years apart. The book is divided into four sections of Colville's war experience—Yorkshire, the Mediterranean, Holland, and Bergen-Belsen—and outlines the young artist's witness to both the horrors and everyday life of the Canadian soldier. It read to me like a travelogue, and a plan quickly formed in my mind: I would travel, exactly seventy-five years

Alex Colville, *The Nijmegen Bridge, Holland*, 1946. Oil on canvas. Beaverbrook Collection of War Art, Canadian War Museum, Ottawa

later, to the sites immortalized in Colville's paintings and reimagine them through my own perspective and artistic medium, the symphony orchestra.

The trip in late August 2019 was transformational. From a ruined and abandoned air base in Driffield, UK, to the roaring cicada choruses on the hills outside of Toulon, from biking through the Dutch countryside to the Groesbeek Canadian War Cemetery, to sitting amongst the gently swaying purple heather at the Bergen-Belsen Memorial in Germany—I could never have imagined how much being in a space would inform the composition of a musical work. I returned with an astounding amount of research, including concrete documents, photos, and firsthand accounts from locals. But more importantly, I returned with an impression of place—of Colville's experience in 1944–45, how the world has changed, and how some things have stayed the same. Over the next couple of years—interrupted, of course, by a pandemic (not entirely a bad thing for a composer who just needs to be chained to his piano)—I wrote *Tracing Colville* for full orchestra, which was premiered by the Kingston Symphony Orchestra in October 2022.

The piece is written in four movements, each best described as a tone poem. Tone poems, which gained prominence in the Late Romantic period through composers like Richard Strauss (*Also Sprach Zarathustra*), Claude Debussy (*Prélude à l'après-midi d'un faune*), and Modest Mussorgsky (*A Night on Bald Mountain*), are compositions that transcend pure music to tell a story or paint a picture.

As an enlisted war artist, Colville was first sent to Yorkshire, England, to practice his artistic skills by observing the men of the Royal Canadian Army Service Corps. They trained to fix vehicles, stall trucks on the lush green hills, and set up field kitchens. This mundane work—seemingly far from the front lines—was infused with the unbridled enthusiasm of eager young people, sometimes naively ready to join the fight. The music of the first movement, *Yorkshire—June, 1944*, takes inspiration from several sources and unabashedly portrays Colville's time there, using musical devices to evoke not only his paintings but also the listener's own perceptions of place. Following an exuberant and jazzy opening, the violins, violas, and cellos play long, smoothly intersecting, undulating lines that aurally represent Yorkshire's rolling hills. Energetic snippets recall the big band music so central to the period, as well as the BBC broadcasts that were a lifeline of information and morale for both Britain and occupied Europe. The movement progresses to the mechanics shop and the industrialization of war, with clanging cowbells and machine-like rhythms. Two whimsical bassoons—a temperament the bassoon is particularly suited to portray—emphasize the sense of fun, camaraderie, and adventure often expressed in the writings of young soldiers at the time. A solo oboe, capable of incredible lyrical beauty, introduces the 'Colville theme', inspired by Vera Lynn's wartime classic, *The White Cliffs of Dover*. The movement ends with an exuberant fanfare as the Allies prepare for the D-Day landings on June 6, 1944. Although Colville wasn't part of that invasion, he soon found himself in an invasion of his own.

'Colville Theme' by Dean Burry, *Tracing Colville*, 2022

In July, Colville was loaned to the Canadian Navy, as their own artists were busy in London completing D-Day works. Two infantry landing ships, the HMCS *Prince Henry* and *Prince David*, were sent to the Mediterranean to assist in Operation Dragoon: the Allied invasion of southern France, which took place on August 15. Aside from the challenges of painting on a ship in rolling seas, Colville's work depicts a visceral, tense, and exciting nighttime invasion of the beaches of Provence. Normandy had been hell-on-earth—what were the Allies sailing into now? My visit to Toulon, literally on the seventy-fifth anniversary of the landing, was the first significant moment when I realized that actually being in these places would drastically affect the sonic world of the orchestral piece.

During a visit to the *Mémorial du débarquement et de la libération de Provence* on Mont Faron, I was captivated by the incredible sound of the local cicadas. The air was charged with their electric buzzing, and I knew then that this sound would have framed that nighttime assault. *Côte d'Azur—August, 1944* begins with a free 'soundscape' that strives to imitate real-world sounds, with each violinist playing the part of a cicada to recreate the Toulon hillside. In the distance, flutes, oboes, clarinets, and bassoons recall a rusty accordion playing Leip and Schultz's *Lili Marleen*—a song that, remarkably, became a source of comfort for both Allied and Axis forces. The cicadas fade, and the invasion begins with an insistent pulse in the lowest range of the marimba, like a beating heart, as the landing craft silently slide through the dark waters to their destination. An explosive orchestral *tutti* and descending string glissandi introduce the brilliance of a German flare (as depicted in one of Colville's notable works). The tempo quickens as the invasion unfolds, with the Colville theme returning as the Allied commandos make their way through the thick coastal brambles. A final flurry of action leads back to the cicadas at dawn, this time accompanied by the thunder of distant artillery.

Spending my first night in Amsterdam offered me a comforting insight: of all the continental European countries, the Netherlands feels the most 'Canadian' to me. It's hard to define, but I think it has to do with the relatively relaxed approach to life, the love and value of nature, and a humbleness despite being surrounded by much more nationally aggressive neighbors. I'm sure that's one of the reasons the two countries

Dean Burry, 2nd movement from *Tracing Colville*, 2022

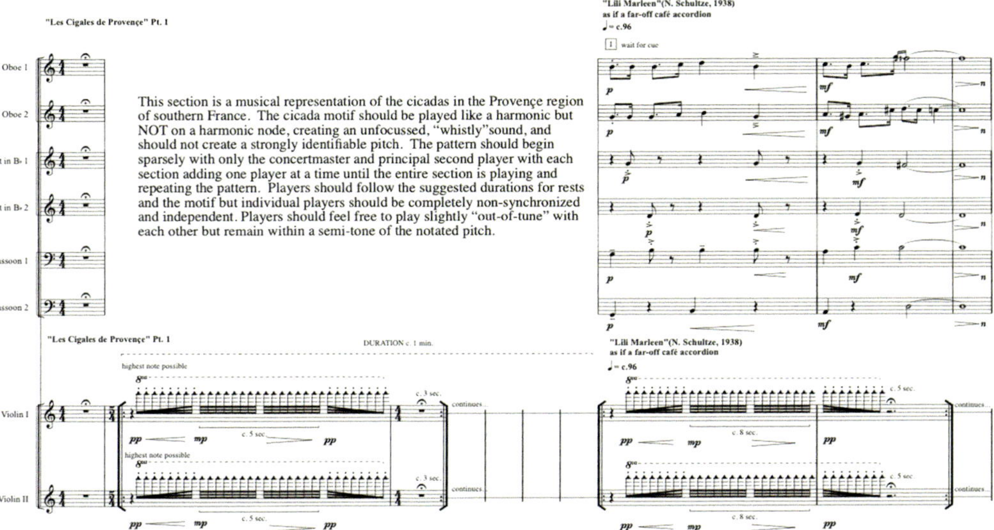

enjoy such a close kinship, even beyond the liberation. Colville created numerous sketches, watercolors, and oils of the iconic Nijmegen Bridge, which played an important role in both the Market Garden and Operation Veritable campaigns. Architecture plays a key role in musical construction, exemplified by the symmetry and balance found in the classical works of Mozart and Haydn. *Nijmegen—November, 1944* begins with an unaccompanied trumpet duet, recalling the mournful *Last Post* bugle calls of military remembrance. This leads to a towering layering of brass, strings, and woodwinds that rise to the strength and grandeur of the bridge itself. A weary trombone solo evokes exhausted infantry along a flooded dyke (Colville's *Infantry Near Nijmegen*), and a final fanfare heralds the liberation of the area. But despite liberation in Nijmegen, the winter of '44 marked the beginning of one of the most horrific periods in Dutch history, as tens of thousands of men, women and children in other parts of the country starved to death during the *Hongerwinter* (the Dutch famine of 1944–1945, also known as the Hunger Winter). The jubilant fanfare is replaced by icy interjections from the violins and violas in their extreme upper registers. An alto saxophone—a rarity in the standard symphony orchestra, but the instrument I grew up playing—begins a plaintive lullaby of a mother singing her dying child to sleep.

This lullaby, repeated and distorted throughout the orchestra, becomes a dissonant and anguished representation of a country in despair. However, like the liberation, there is hope. This pain is interrupted by tubular bells playing *Het Wilhelmus*, the Dutch national anthem. Again, visiting Nijmegen in person proved invaluable. While sitting on a park bench at the north end of the bridge, I heard a church carillon begin to chime across the Waal River. This was followed by another carillon in Lent behind me (you can see the steeple in Colville's *Nijmegen Bridge*) and then a third in Nijmegen. In Colville's war report, he writes of how certain images and shades of color in the sky inspired him. As a composer, my inspiration frequently comes from the sounds around me. The anthem is joined by two other tubular bell players positioned at the back of the theater: one playing *O Canada*, the national anthem of Canada, and the other my Colville theme. The gesture literally rings out the enduring connection between the two countries—songs of liberation heard in music that was always present but now held new meaning. Yet, as Colville painted the destruction of dykes, ruined churches, and fields, he had only begun to witness the depths of human destruction.

'How in the world can I portray the horrors of the Bergen-Belsen Concentration Camp?' I remember this echoing through my mind as I walked through the haunting yet beautiful forest clearing on Lunenburg Heath. Colville was driven to Bergen-Belsen on April 28, 1945, two weeks after the camp had been liberated. Over 50,000 people had died there, mostly of disease and starvation, including Anne Frank and her sister Margot, who perished just weeks before the camp was turned over to British and Canadian soldiers by its German administrators. In 2019, I premiered an opera called *Shanawdithit*, written with Algonquin First Nation librettist Yvette Nolan. The opera told the story of the last known member of the Beothuk Nation, who died in my home province of Newfoundland and Labrador in 1829. Nolan's libretto avoided the trope of the 'dead female' at the end of the opera, instead celebrating Shanawdithit through her artwork, legacy, and (according to modern genealogy) descendants. This Indigenous way of working informed my approach to *Bergen-Belsen—April 1945*, which celebrates the lives of the many survivors and victims of the camp. The Colville theme, now treated as a meditative bass line, is presented eighteen times—the number eighteen in Hebrew is *chai*, meaning 'life'. Above this repeating pattern, the instruments of the orchestra bring to life the children, lovers, parents, elders, teachers, builders, thinkers, healers, artists, leaders, and celebrations that must never be forgotten, guiding us beyond the nightmare of the Holocaust. The solo oboe, once again playing the Colville theme, is joined by a single bassoon, suggesting the loss of one of the soldiers from Yorkshire. The piece ends with a gentle yet unsettled sense that although the war has ended, its effects will linger on.

Symphonies and songs may seem quite different. They are played in different places, for different purposes, and frequently for different audiences. But in truth, they draw strength from the same magic: the sublime ability of music to conjure joy, despair, elation, and resolve. Both reflect back to us the human emotions that are heightened in times of war, through experiences of defeat, endurance, resistance, and liberation.

5
RECORDING LIBERATION SONGS: SONIC BRIDGES

Frank Mehring

While one can analyze, arrange, and contextualize music, its true essence is only fully grasped through performance, listening, and, in the case of dance, viewing. To truly connect with music on a visceral level, to feel its emotional power, it must be experienced in its intended form. The tracks included on the original CD accompanying the Dutch edition of this book, *De Soundtrack van de Bevrijding* (2015), along with the videos available on the Canadian Tulip Festival website, represent performances that had, for the most part, never been recorded before.

These liberation songs were brought to life by artists from both sides of the Dutch–German border, who sang and danced in the Anton van Duinkerken Hall at Radboud University, the Freedom Museum in Groesbeek, and the Joseph Beuys Gesamtschule in Kleve, Germany. These performances were part of the commemorations for Operation Market Garden in September 1944 and the liberation in May 1945.

I extend my deepest gratitude to the singers, dancers, musicians, teachers, and students who made this concert series possible. May the spirit of freedom and liberation continue to inspire us all, especially the younger generations, helping to bridge divides and foster our shared desire for freedom and mutual understanding.

1. **Gerhard Winkler** (1906–1977)
   Wees maar gerust (Günther Schwenn/ Dutch: Hand Dunk) (1943)
2. **Atma Kenswil** (1892–1985)
   Praeludium Pacis for solo piano (1945)
3. **Felix Kwast** (1889–1949)
   Theme song from: Arnhem Concerto for solo piano (1944)
4. **Norbert Schultze** (1911–2002)
   Onder de Lantaren—Lili Marleen (Herre de Vos) (1939)
5. **Kees Sommer**
   Tommy Song (Meimaand 1945)

6. **Leo Fredriks**
   De Sten Gun Walk (Daan Hooykaas) (1945)
7. **Jack Bulterman** (1909–1977)
   Snoezepoes (Text and Musik) (1940)
8. **Frank Fox** (1902–1965)
   Amerika hat Rhythmus und Wien hat Melodie
   (Erich Meder/English: Ezra Lapides) (1945)
9. **Fredy Salter**
   Ik kan niet swingen (Bob Wallagh) (1946)
10. **Louis Noiret** (1896–1968)
   America, We Thank You (ca. 1949) (G. Bon en H. Joosten)
11. **Barend Renden** (1850–1923)
   Bevrijdingslied 1945 (Barend Renden)
12. **Jan van Weelden** (1917–1992)
   Vrede (5 Mei 1945) (Ph. M. van Kranenburg) (1945)
13. **Johan Sluijter**
   Het vrije Nederland (Herre de Vos)
   Bevrijdingslied 1940–1945
14. **Albert de Booy** (1897–1971)
   Trees heeft een Canadees (Lou de Groot) (1945)

Several online video recordings by pianist Jens Barnieck, alongside vocalists Saskia Bak, Sarah Konig, Joost Huijs, and Frank Mehring, were created to celebrate the 2020 Canadian Tulip Festival. This festival, deeply rooted in the history of the Dutch liberation during World War II, is typically a major public event in Canada's capital, Ottawa, Ontario. Held among 300,000 blooming tulips, the festival honors a tradition that began when HRH Princess Margriet was born in Ottawa during the war. Following the German surrender to Canadian forces on May 5, 1945, Queen Wilhelmina sent 100,000 tulip bulbs as a 'thank you' gift to Canada's capital.

Due to the COVID-19 pandemic, live events were not possible in 2020. Instead, the organizers of the 68th edition of the Canadian Tulip Festival transitioned the celebration to an online platform. All performances, programming, and public participation were made available digitally, allowing the festival to continue celebrating the 75th anniversary of the Liberation of the Netherlands with Canadians and a global audience through their website, social media, and a new YouTube channel. Festival President Grant Hooker invited Frank Mehring to collaborate on this virtual event, ensuring that the tradition of celebrating with music remained vibrant despite the challenges of the pandemic.

The results can be viewed here: Songs of Liberation—Canadian Tulip Festival. The introductory video featured the following announcement:

> I am interested in tracing how music can function as a key to the past and create strong ties between people, places, and nations. In May of 1945, you would have seen a very different Nijmegen than the city outside my doors this afternoon. May 5, 1945 saw the surrender of Nazi soldiers who had occupied the Netherlands since 1940 to Canadian General Charles Foulkes, Commander of the 1st Canadian Army, in the city of Wageningen. It was the end of a torturous 5-year period in this country's history and the Dutch people celebrated their liberation with dances, songs, and cheers. In the summer that followed that wonderful day in May, there were more than 300 songs published in the Netherlands celebrating the country's release from bondage. So many of these songs rang out across the country that they were labeled by the Dutch as 'bevrijdingsliederen'—'Songs of Liberation'. I've captured the history of many of these songs in a Dutch-language book first printed in 2015. Each day of this year's Canadian Tulip Festival, from Friday, May 8th through Monday, May 18th, I or my associate, Jens Barnieck, will introduce you to a new 'Song of Liberation' on the Festival's TulipTV YouTube channel. Mr. Barnieck, the pianist in all the recordings you'll hear, and I will put each song into musical and historical context. Dutch lyrics will be presented by means of English and French subtitles and the music will be accompanied by images that will bring the songs and the times that led to their creation to life. Recent global struggles against a common threat to our health bring to mind the global struggles that led to the May 1945 victory by Canadians in the Netherlands. We can be grateful today for the leadership and public cooperation that we know will lead us to a return to our normal lives. The Dutch are ever grateful to Canada for the sacrifices they made in 1944 and 1945 that allowed the people of this European country to return to their normal lives… and to freedom. Thank you Canada!'

FESTIVAL INFO ⌄ COMMEMORATE ⌄ RESOURCES ⌄ CONTACT ⌄ ADOPT A TULIP CANADIAN TULIP FESTIVAL HOODIES

Songs of Liberation

Iosted by Professor Frank Mehring

rank Mehring, professor of American Studies at Radboud University, Iijmegen. He teaches 20th and 21st century visual culture and music, heories of popular culture, transnational modernism, and processes of ultural translation in Euro-American contexts. In his book, "The Soundtrack of Liberation", Dr. Mehring researched and presented 300 ongs by Dutch Composers in the summer of 1945.

lease view the series introduction (to the right) then enjoy the individual erformances below.

VISIT TULIPTV ON YOUTUBE

Liberation Songs overview at Canadian Tulip Festival Website

CONCLUSION

Frank Mehring

This book offers an in-depth multimedia exploration of how Dutch liberation songs and music shaped the cultural memory of liberation and recovery, emphasizing the power of music in overcoming oppression and celebrating newfound freedom in a transatlantic context. By analyzing visual and cultural references in cover art, multilingual lyrics, and diverse musical genres, it becomes evident that Dutch artists and civilians embraced liberation with joy, music, and dance. Many songs, particularly marches, convey profound gratitude for the heroism of the Allied forces.

While cultural memory often highlights the contributions of British and American armed forces, the sheet music also underscores the critical role of Canadian troops in the liberation and subsequent peacebuilding efforts after World War II. These cultural sources provide a fresh perspective of how Dutch citizens welcomed the presence of Canadian soldiers. However, interactions were not always harmonious, as tensions occasionally arose due to moral lapses, a burgeoning black-market economy, and competition between Dutch men and Canadian liberators for the affections of Dutch women.

The sheet music reflects a pivotal moment in Dutch history when an entire generation grappled with the loss and recovery of freedom, as well as the challenge of preserving and commemorating liberty.

Returning to the beginning of this book, Crosby, Stills, Nash, and Young's song about freedom, *Find the Cost of Freedom*, serves as a powerful metaphor for the human toll of war and occupation. The song's somber call to 'lay your body down' underscores the ultimate sacrifice made by those who gave their lives for freedom, resonating deeply with the Dutch experience of loss and resilience. Similarly, Canadian poet Earle Birney encapsulated this spirit in his war poem *On the Road to Nijmegen.* In the final stanza, he vividly portrays the hardships faced by Canadian soldiers as they pushed through floods, barren trees, and freezing conditions to bring freedom to the Dutch–German border:

So peering through sleet as we neared Nijmegen
I glimpsed the rainbow arch of your eyes
Over the clank of the jeep
Your quick grave laughter
Outrising at last the rockets
Brought me what spells I repeat
As I travel this road
That arrives at not future
And wat creed I can bring
To our daily crimes
To this guilt
In the griefs of the old
And the graves of the young.

This book on *Liberation Songs* has been written at a time when war has once again erupted in Europe. For my generation, which grew up during the longest period of peace in the heart of Europe and experienced the fall of the Berlin Wall as teenagers, the resurgence of conflict is almost inconceivable. Yet here we are, struggling to comprehend the unimaginable.

The return of war to our continent serves as a stark reminder of the fragility of peace. Our collective memories are imbued with the optimism of the post-Cold War era, making today's hostilities particularly jarring.

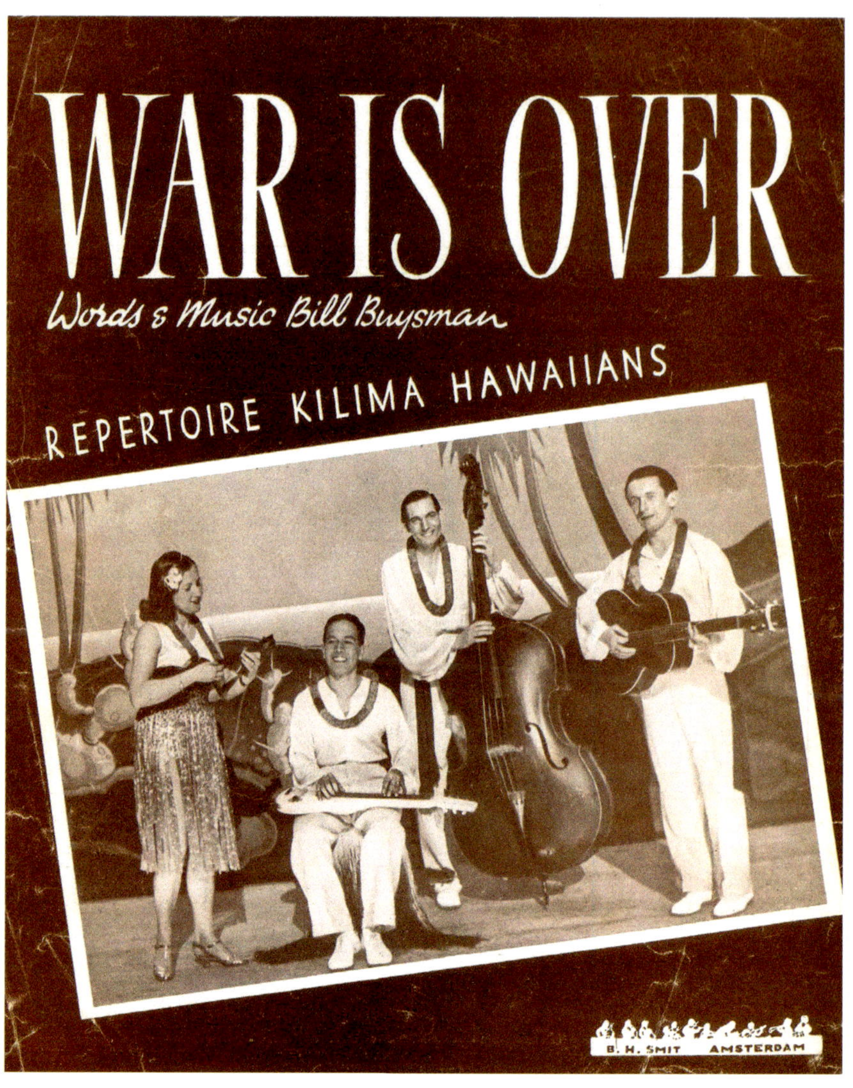

War is over, cover (1945)

In documenting these liberation songs, I am reminded of the enduring power of music to unite, inspire, and provide solace during times of turmoil. The songs in this book reflect the resilience and spirit of those who faced immense challenges during World War II on both sides of the Atlantic. They stand as a testament to the unyielding human pursuit of freedom.

As a German fortunate to work with young people at a university in the Netherlands, I feel particular pain when speaking with friends and colleagues in Ukraine, near the Russian border. Former friends and neighbors have become enemies, embroiled in a conflict that has torn apart lives and communities. How many songs will it take, and how many generations must embrace the unifying power of music to rebuild trust and friendship, as the Dutch and Germans have done in the heart of Europe over the last 80 years?

As Bob Dylan sang, 'The answer, my friend, is blowin' in the wind.' Yet we can remain hopeful that by cherishing freedom and joining hands, as the activists of the civil rights movement once did, we too can overcome. *We shall live in peace.* Indeed, there is a sonic silver lining on the horizon for those willing to embrace it.

In our common struggle for freedom,
Songs arise not only as weapons in war
But also as melodies of healing,
Bridging national divides to celebrate liberation,
Echoing the resounding chorus of
Peace to All and *War is Over*,
Harmonizing to restore and strengthen
The meanings of liberty and democracy
And to find the *Cost of Freedom.*
So, *Sing your Song of Thanks* and dance the *Sten-Gun Walk.*
Jump into action for freedom today,
Across cultures—with all and for all.
Eens komt weer de dag van de VREDE!
Let Freedom Ring.

CODA: FOURTEEN LIBERATION SONGS

Jens Barnieck

The Transatlantic Soundtrack of Freedom draws from a rich collection of Dutch liberation songs amassed by Hugo Keesing over the past decades. The fourteen songs featured in this compilation, with their lyrics reprinted here, capture the spirit and emotions of the Dutch people during the pivotal days of liberation. Jens Barnieck has provided brief but insightful introductions to each song, offering context and enhancing the reader's understanding of their significance.

What sets this collection apart is the inclusion of newly recorded performances, accessible on the Canadian Tulip Festival's website. Many of these songs had never been recorded before, making these renditions a valuable and unique contribution to the preservation of this important cultural heritage. These recordings offer listeners a rare opportunity to experience the music that uplifted and united the Netherlands during a time of profound change, ensuring that these songs, and the stories they tell, continue to resonate with future generations.

A singer of the United Service Organizations (USO) entertains troops of a U.S. armored division near Geldrop in the Netherlands. NIOD

Gerhard Winkler (1906–1977) was a renowned German composer known for his work in 'Schlager' (popular songs) and film music. Among his notable compositions are the beloved *Caprifischer* from 1943 and the scores for the 'Schwarzwald' films produced after the war. The Dutch song *Wees maar gerust* is based on one of Winkler's compositions, with a Dutch translation by the composer and lyricist Han Dunk (1909–1996). The original German song, titled *Ich bin dir treu. Ein Brief aus der Heimat,* bore the subtitle 'The resounding field mail of Radio Belgrade', a slogan aimed at German soldiers during the war. The sheet music for this piece was first published in 1942, featuring a cover image of the famed singer Lale Andersen (1905–1972). The cover exudes comfort and reassurance. The soft green hues and elegant script reflect a soothing, sentimental tone. A ribbon-wrapped letter looks like a present and promises loyalty and calm in Dutch, complemented by a German translation. The smiling woman in fur, framed in a photo, symbolizes joy and elegance. Featuring Dick Willebrandts' dance orchestra and vocalist Hellie Verschuur, the design highlights postwar optimism, romance, and the charm of a slow foxtrot era.

Wees maar gerust, cover (1943)

WEES MAAR GERUST

Music: Gerhard Winkler / German lyrics: Günther Schwenn
Dutch lyrics: Han Dunk / Year of publication: 1943

Vele brieven heb jij geschreven,
Ver van 't vaderland naar je huis.
Steeds zijn je gedachten gebleven,
Bij al wat je achterliet thuis.
Dominerend in heel je denken
Is de vraag hoe of het mij gaat.
Nooit wil j'aan je zelf eens aandacht schenken.
Daarom dat 'k je thans weten laat:

Refrein:
Wees maar gerust, maak j' over mij geen zorgen!
Ik blijf je trouw daar kan je van op aan.
Net als het was blijft het ook nu en morgen:
'n Ander dan jij zal nooit voor mij bestaan.
Keer jij straks weer na al die bange dagen,
Dan wordt het leven een waar paradijs!
Mag het dan nu wat moeilijk zijn te dragen,
Wees maar gerust, 't gaat alles weer voorbij.
Jij komt terug en blijft voor goed bij mij.

Jij moet al zoo heel veel verdragen.
Zooveel zorgen en zoo'n verdriet.
'k Zou er niet aan denken te klagen.
Mijn leed zinkt daarbij in het niet.
Eenmaal zal een eind zijn gekomen
Aan dit alles, en dan daarna
Zullen wij van ons geluk slechts droomen!
Moge die tijd komen weldra!

Refrein

PLEASE REST ASSURED[119]

So many letters you have written,
Far from the homeland to your home.
Always your thoughts remained,
At all that you left behind at home.
Dominating all your thoughts
Is the question of how I am doing.
Never once do you want to pay attention to yourself.
That's why I now let you know:

Chorus:
Please rest assured!
I'll stay true to you, you can be sure of that.
Just as it was it will remain now and tomorrow:
Other than you will never exist for me.
Soon you will return after all those anxious days,
Life will be a true paradise!
If it's a little hard to bear now,
Please rest assured it will all pass again.
You will come back and stay with me for good.

You already have so much to bear.
So much worry and sorrow.
I wouldn't think of complaining.
My suffering is nothing compared to that.
Once there will be an end
To all this, and then
We shall only dream of our happiness!
May that time come soon!

Chorus

Atma Kenswil (1892–1985) was a composer known for her religiously and philosophically inspired 'mysteries of sound', which she wove into her songs, piano pieces, and chamber music. Her compositions often drew on the melodic and rhythmic elements of religious and folk music, creating a unique blend that resonated with deeper spiritual themes.

For the CD accompanying the original book *Soundtrack van de Bevrijding*, the artists took the creative liberty of incorporating the poem *Conversation* by Frances Angermayer of Kansas City into the extended pauses of Kenswil's piano piece. Written and released in 1943, this poem, in its bilingual version from the Hugo Keesing collection, is dedicated to Field Marshal Montgomery: 'In memory of those who laid down their lives for the liberation of Holland.' The composer described the piece as a 'vocal depiction of the tragedy of partial liberation', capturing the somber and reflective tone of the poem within the music. The cover is minimalist and elegant, reflecting a solemn tone. Its clean, sepia-toned design and graceful typography suggest tranquility and reflection. Likely composed to mark liberation, the piece symbolizes peace and freedom through its simple yet profound presentation for piano.

Paeludium Pacis, cover (1945)

PRAELUDIUM PACIS FOR PIANO, INCLUDING 'CONVERSATION'

Music: Atma Kenswil / Lyrics ('Conversation'): Frances Angermayer
Year of publication: 1945 (Praeludium Pacis) en 1943 ('Conversation')

Look God, I have never spoken to You,
But now I want to say 'how do You do'
You see God, they told me You didn't exist,
and like a fool, I believed all this.

Last night from a shell hole, I saw Your sky,
I figured right then they had told me a lie.
Had I taken the time to see things You made,
I'd have known they weren't calling a spade a spade.

I wonder, God, if You'd shake my hand,
Somehow I feel that You will understand.
Funny, I had to come to this hellish place,
Before I had time to see Your face.

Well, I guess there isn't much more to say,
But I'm sure glad, God, I met You today.
I guess the 'zero-hour' will soon be here,
But I'm not afraid since I know You're near.

The signal! Well, God, I'll have to go,
I like You lots, this I want You to know.
Look now, this will be a horrible fight,
Who knows, I may come to Your house tonight.

Though I wasn't friendly to You before,
I wonder God, If You'll wait at Your door.
Look, I'm crying. Me shedding tears,
I wish I had known You these many years.

Well, I have to go now, God, good-bye,
Strange, since I met You, I'm not afraid to die.

■ Willem Felix Kwast (1889–1949) was born into a deeply musical family. He was the son of the Dutch conductor Jan Albert Kwast from Arnhem and the nephew of the renowned composer and pedagogue James Kwast. His *Arnhem Concerto,* composed for solo piano, is dedicated to the paratroopers of 1944, with the inscription: 'May their names always live on. In memory of the fallen paratroopers.' The cover pays tribute to the airborne soldiers of 1944 during Operation Market Garden. It features a dramatic scene of soldiers advancing, with bold red, black, and yellow tones underscoring urgency and conflict. A paratrooper takes center stage, rifle in hand, silhouetted against the Arnhem bridge—symbolizing the battle's historical significance. The dynamic, energetic style conveys heroism, resilience, and sacrifice. This powerful design honors the bravery of the Allied forces in the liberation of Arnhem.

Arnhem Concerto, cover (1945)

ARNHEM CONCERTO

Music: Felix Kwast / *Year of publication*: 1944

The airborne troops,
Having just landed,
Are going to give their lives
For liberation and freedom…

Marching and fighting
To the bridge across the river Rhine…
They meet with severe resistance from the enemy…
Bridge blown up and numerous soldiers,
Filled and wounded.

Thanks of our nation
To the heroes,
Who lost the battle of Arnhem,
But won the war.

Norbert Schultze (1911–2002) was the composer of the second and most famous version of *Lili Marleen* (1938). The first version of Hans Leip's poem was set to music by Rudolf Zink in 1937, but both versions were sung by Lale Andersen. Andersen first met Schultze in Berlin in 1932, when he was performing with the student cabaret group *Die Vier Nachrichter* from Munich. In his autobiography, Schultze wrote, 'It became a symbol of homesickness, abandonment, and sadness (...), but above all, of hope and the promise of coming home again.' The song was translated into many languages, with English versions featuring slight variations in the spelling of the name *Lili.* The cover features a stylish, windswept woman standing under a glowing lantern, evoking romantic nostalgia. The iconic WWII song *Lili Marleen* reflects longing and love during wartime, often associated with soldiers far from home. The bold red and white palette adds drama, while dynamic typography and flowing lines highlight movement and emotional intensity. This design captures the song's bittersweet mood and enduring cultural impact during the 1940s.

Onder de Lantaren. Lili Marleen, cover (1939)

ONDER DE LANTAREN: LILI MARLEEN

Music: Norbert Schultze / *Dutch lyrics*: Herre de Vos
Year of publication: 1939

Onder de lantaren, bij de groote poort,
vrijen vele paren bij avond ongestoord…
Als ik van boord kom, ga 'k meteen,
terstond naar die lantaren heen,
met jou, Lili Marleen, met jou, Lili Marleen!

Onder de lantaren, heel dicht bij elkaar…
dat verliefd wij waren, zag wel een ieder daar!
En elk die glimlacht, naar ik meen,
gaat hij langs die lantaren heen:
Om ons, Lili Marleen, om ons, Lili Marleen!

Onder de lantaren, werd een sein gehoord
dat kwam van de baren en riep mij weer aan boord!
Ik zei vaarwel en ging toen heen.
bij de lantaren stond alleen
mijn schat, Lili Marleen, mijn schat, Lili Marleen!

Onder de lantaren, loop jij nu, mijn kind…
ik ben weer gaan varen en zwalk door weer en wind.
Soms is mijn hart zoo zwaar als steen.
en dan gaan mijn gedachten heen
naar jou, Lili Marleen, naar jou, Lili Marleen!

LILI MARLENE

Music: Norbert Schultze, arranged by Helmy Kresa
English Lyrics: Tommie Connor (1941)

Underneath the lantern, by the barrack gate,
Darling, I remember the way you used to wait
'Twas there that you whispered tenderly,
That you'd love me, You'd always be.
My Lili of the lamplight, My own Lili Marlene.

Time would come for roll call, Time for us to part,
Darling I'd caress you and press you to my heart.
And there 'neath that far off lantern light,
I'd hold you tight, We'd kiss 'Good night.'
My Lili of the lamplight, My own Lili Marlene.

Orders came for sailing somewhere over there,
All confined to barracks was more than I could bear.
I knew you were waiting in the street,
I heard your feeet, but could not meet.
My Lili of the lamplight, My own Lili Marlene.

Resting in a billet, just behind the line,
Even though we're parted, your lips are close to mine,
You wait where that lantern softly gleams,
Your sweet face seems to haunt my dreams.
My Lili of the lamplight, My own Lili Marlene.

LILI MARLENE

Music: Norbert Schultze
American version: Mack David

Would you like to hear the story
Of a girl that many soldiers know
It's a tale of love and all its glory
They tell when the lights are soft and low.
Underneath the lamppost by the barrack gate,
Standing all alone, every night you'll see her wait.
She waits for a boy who marched away
And though he's gone she hears him say,
'Oh, promise you'll be true,
Fare thee well, Lili Marlene.
Till I return to you,
Fare thee well, Lili Marlene.'

With a kiss she gave her promise
To be constant as the stars above.
Ev'ry soldier knows she's kept her promise
And she has been faithful to her love.

Underneath the lamppost by the barrack gate,
Standing all alone, every night you'll see her wait.
For this is the place a vow was made,
And breezes sing her serenade.
'Oh, promise you'll be true,
Fare thee well, Lili Marlene.
Till I return to you,
Fare thee well, Lili Marlene.'

Summer soon gave way to Autumn
Then came Winter with his snow-white beard.
Once again she faced a lonely Springtime.
But night after night she still appeared.

Underneath the lamppost by the barrack gate,
Standing all alone, every night you'll see her wait.
And there in the lamplight it is said,
A halo shines above her head.
'Oh, promise you'll be true,
Fare thee well, Lili Marlene.
Till I return to you,
Fare thee well, Lili Marlene.'
Tho' each tale must have an ending
No one know just what the end will be.
But tonight when twilight is descending
If you'll come along,
Here's what you'll see:

Underneath the lamppost by the barrack gate,
Standing all alone, every night you'll see her wait.
And as they go marching to the fray,
The soldiers all salute and say,
'We'll tell him you've been true,
Fare thee well, Lili Marlene.
Till he returns to you,
Fare thee well, Lili Marlene.'

■ Little is known about the composer Kees Sommer at this time. The cover of *Tommy Song* describes it as a 'March (Two-step)' and notes that it was sung by Miss Marianne van den Bergh. The English lyrics of *Tommy Song* express gratitude for the liberation and mention several key figures who contributed to it: '(...) Eisenhower, Patch, Patton, Montgomery, Hodges, Dempsey, Simpson. They will remain in history (...)'. The cover celebrates the joy of liberation in May 1945. A lively scene shows cheering Dutch civilians atop an Allied tank, waving Dutch, American, and British flags in gratitude for their freedom. Two fleeing caricatured German soldiers symbolize the end of Nazi occupation. The illustration conveys jubilation, victory, and unity through bold blue and red tones. The playful energy and patriotic imagery highlight postwar celebration and Allied heroism in liberating the Netherlands. This song must have brought the composer a certain fame and popularity, since another of Summer's songs, *Canuck Song*, dedicated to the Canadian troops in Holland, May 1945 shows on the cover sheet 'Words and Music by the composer of the *Tommy Song*, Kees Sommer.

Tommy Song, cover (1945)

TOMMY SONG

Music and lyrics: Kees Sommer
Year of publication: 1945

Ev'ry one is smiling,
Ev'rything O.K.
'Cause the Allied forces
swept the German troops away.
Flags again are flying
in a cleaner sky
Happy days of peace for us
are coming by and by.
The names of Eisenhower, Patch and
Patton and Montgomery.
Hodges, Dempsey, Simpson
they remains [sic] in history.
Now the suns is shining
Holland is now Free.
Therefore let us sing
this little Tommy Melody:

Refrein:
Tommy, how do you do?
Tommy, glad to see you.
There were mighty German fortifications
You destroyed them and therefore
our best congratulations.
We knew Hitler's command:
'They may only nine hours stay.'

Churchill did understand
and all was right O.K.
Churchill in een bootje
auf dem schönen Rhein,
Kinder das ist wunderbar...
zu schön um wahr zu sein.

Churchill wijst naar 't oosten
with his big cigar.
En hij zegt 'Montgomery,
zeg, zie je dat wel daar?
Duizenden soldaten
Trekken naar het Oosten,
wat een reuze druk verkeer
zonder ransel of geweer!'
Was soll das bedeuten?
Was mag das wohl sein?
Das ist einfach 'fabelhaft'.
Das war die Wacht am Rhein.

Refrein:
Tommy, how do you do?
Tommy, glad to meet you.
Dank je zeer voor alles wat je presteerde
En dat je de moffen nu eens danig mores leerde.
't Is nu uit met terreur
en met Nazi-dwinglandij.
Tommy, thank you so much
want nu is Holland vrij.

TOMMY SONG

Ev'ry one is smiling,
Ev'rything O.K.
'Cause the Allied forces
swept the German troops away.
Flags again are flying
in a cleaner sky
Happy days of peace for us
are coming by and by.
The names of Eisenhower, Patch and
Patton and Montgomery.
Hodges, Dempsey, Simpson
they remain in history.

Now the suns is shining
Holland is now Free.
Therefore let us sing
this little Tommy Melody:

Chorus:
Tommy, how do you do?
Tommy, glad to see you.
There were mighty German fortifications
You destroyed them and therefore
our best congratulations.
We knew Hitler's command:
'They may only nine hours stay.'

Churchill did understand
and all was right O.K.
Churchill in a little boat
On the beautiful Rhine,
Children this is wonderful...
too good to be true.
Churchill points east
with his big cigar.
And he says 'Montgomery,
say, do you see that over there?
Thousands of soldiers
Are moving east,
what a great rush
Without knapsack or rifle!'
What does that mean?
What might that be?
It's simply 'fabulous'.
That was the 'Wacht am Rhein'.

Chorus:
Tommy, how do you do?
Tommy, glad to meet you.

Thank you very much for all you've accomplished
And for teaching the Krauts a good lesson.
It's over with terror
and Nazi coercion.
Tommy, thank you so much
because now Holland is free.

■ Leo Fredriks, a Dutch pianist and author, collaborated with composer and humorist Daan Hooykaas (1913–1982) to create the song *The Sten-Gun Walk: The Social Dance for 1945*. The song was written for Pierre Zom, head of a dance school in Rotterdam, who choreographed the dance steps to accompany it. Fredriks, also known as Fred Riks, had played piano for lessons at the dance school for many years. It was only after the war that he discovered Zom had been active in the resistance and that dozens of machine guns had been hidden beneath the dance school's floor during the occupation. The cover combines postwar celebration with military symbolism. It depicts a couple performing a stylized dance, holding Sten guns like props, blending lighthearted entertainment with references to the weapons of liberation. Behind them, the Dutch flag waves proudly, symbolizing national pride and freedom in 1945. In the background, silhouettes of soldiers and windmills evoke wartime resilience and Dutch identity. The bold typography and vibrant red, white, and blue palette emphasize victory, joy, and cultural rebirth through dance.

De 'Sten-Gun Walk', cover (1945)

DE 'STEN-GUN WALK'

Music: Leo Fredriks / *Lyrics*: Daan Hooykaas
Year of publication: 1945

Oorlogstijd,
Narigheid.
Stil verzet,
Opgelet!
Vliegend over stad en dorpen,
Wapens uitgeworpen.
'Dropping ploeg',
Kreeg genoeg.
Holland vrij!
Ieder blij.
En heel het Nederlandsche volk,
Danst nu de 'Sten-gun walk'.

Refrein:
Hold your sten!
Pas op je tellen!
Hold your sten!
Tred niet versnellen!
Als je een beweging ziet...
Vinger aan de trekker:
'Sta, of 'k schiet!'
Kijk goed uit!
Wees op je hoede!
Kijk goed uit!
Mocht je vermoeden.
Dat je een beweging ziet...
Vinger aan de trekker:
'Sta, of 'k schiet!'
Er's geen vijand in de buurt,
Kom waag dus gauw een kans.
Heden wordt er niet gevuurd,
Dans nu de 'Sten-gun' dans!

STOP

Hold your sten!
Pas op je tellen!
Hold your sten!
Tred niet versnellen!
Als je een beweging ziet…
Vinger aan de trekker:
'Sta, of 'k schiet!'

THE 'STEN-GUN WALK'

Wartime,
Hardship.
Silent Resistance,
Attention!
Flying over town and villages,
Weapons thrown out.
Dropping squad,
Got enough.
Holland free!
Every one happy.
And all the Dutch people,
Now dance the 'Sten-gun walk'.

Chorus:
Hold your sten!
Watch your step!
Hold your sten!
Don't speed up your tread!
If you see any movement…
Finger on the trigger:
'Stand, or I'll shoot!'
Watch carefully!
Be on your guard!
Watch carefully!
Should you suspect

That you see a movement...
Finger on the trigger:
'Stand, or I'll shoot!'
There's no enemy around,
So come take a chance.
Today there's no fire,
Now dance the Sten-gun dance!
STOP

Hold your sten!
Watch your step!
Hold your sten!
Don't speed up your step!
When you see a movement...
Finger on the trigger:
'Stand, or I'll shoot!

Jack Bulterman (1909–1977) was a versatile Dutch musician, excelling as a trumpeter, pianist, arranger, songwriter, conductor, and producer. He gained prominence while touring extensively with his band, The Ramblers. In the late 1940s, Bulterman shifted his focus to working as a producer and arranger, collaborating with well-known artists like The Blue Diamonds, Anneke Grönloh, and Willy Alberti. The cover blends Dutch cultural identity with mid-20th-century entertainment. Dominated by red and white tones, it features a smiling Dutch woman in traditional attire, standing confidently with a windmill—a classic symbol of the Netherlands—in the background. The title, playfully suggesting charm, evokes a cheerful, nostalgic tone. The song, a foxtrot with guitar accompaniment by Jack Bulterman and performed by The Ramblers Orchestra, reflects postwar joy, cultural pride, and the lighthearted music of the era.

Snoezepoes, cover (1945)

SNOEZEPOES

Music and lyrics: Jack Bulterman
Year of publication: 1940

By an old Dutch mill
we were sitting hand in hand;
I whispered tender words,
that she didn't understand,
And I'll never forget,
tho' the years pass away,
The lovely word for 'sweetheart'
I learned that day:

'Snoezepoes!' Snoezepoes!
There by the old Dutch mill,
How I like your wooden shoes
And your smile I remember still!
I met her on a bench
near a linden tree,
And she said to me
that her heart was free...
Snoezepoes! Snoezepoes!
Little girl with your wooden shoes!

Frank Fox (1902–1965) was an orchestra conductor who began his career with the touring international dance orchestra *Wiener Tanzorchester* before relocating to Berlin after Austria's annexation. In Berlin, he served as conductor at the Metropol-Theater and composed music for operettas as well as for over 25 popular films of the time, including *Im weißen Rößl* (1935) and *Schwarzwaldmädel* (1950). The Austrian author Erich Meder (1897–1966) collaborated extensively with Frank Fox but also wrote for other composers, such as Gerhard Winkler. Meder was particularly known for crafting lyrics for Viennese songs. The cover highlights cultural contrasts and harmony between America and Vienna. Depicted are towering American skyscrapers representing modernity and rhythm, paired with Vienna's traditional silhouette of St. Stephen's Cathedral, symbolizing melody and classical culture. The bold red and white design reflects a fusion of styles, while the foxtrot genre underscores postwar musical exchange. The typography and layout exude energy, celebrating transatlantic cultural connections and contrasts through music, rhythm, and melody in 1940s Europe.

America Has Rhythm and Wien hat Melodie, cover (1945)

AMERICA HAS RHYTHM AND WIEN HAT MELODIE

Music: Frank Fox / *English lyrics*: Ezra Lapides
German lyrics: Erich Meder / *Year of publication*: 1945

First there rang out Viennese music
over oceans wide
and Uncle Sam of the U.S.A.
has taken it in stride.
As revenge he started writing
Rhythms very strange
and said to Wien:
ours sounds so nice
how would you like to change?

Chorus:
America has rhythm
and 'Wien hat Melodie'.
My heart dances right with them
cause I'm in love
with both of them you see.
Sweet music makes me swing out,
'bout that I cannot lie
and so we raise our praises to the sky.
America has tempo
and Wien Gemütlichkeit.
In New York speed is needed,
but Wien has time that's right.
America has rhythm
and loads of energy
and 'Wien hat Melodie'.

Einst erklangen Wiener Weisen
übern grossen Teich,
und Onkel Sam aus U.S.A.
gefiel die Sache gleich.
Als Revanche drauf

spielt er Rhythmen,
Vindobona lauscht
und sagt ihm dann,
das klingt so nett,
wie wär's,
wenn man tauscht?

Chorus

Sitzt die Mitzi mit dem Jonny
auf der Bank im Park,
den Arm in Arm, den Mund an Mund
und dunkel wird es stark.
Mitzi singt was, Jonny peift was,
bald hört man nichts mehr
und so erwacht im schönen Wien
der Fremdenverkehr.

Chorus:

AMERICA HAS RHYTHM AND VIENNA HAS MELODY

First there rang out Viennese Music
over oceans wide
and Uncle Sam of the U.S.A.
has taken it in stride.
As revenge he started writing
Rhythms very strange
and said to Vienna:
ours sounds so nice
how would you like to change?

Chorus:
America has rhythm
and 'Vienna has melody'.
My heart dances right with them
cause I'm in love

with both of them you see.
Sweet music makes me swing out,
'bout that I cannot lie
and so we raise our praises to the sky.
America has tempo
and Vienna Gemütlichkeit.
In New York speed is needed,
but Vienna has time that's right.
America has rhythm
and loads of energy
and 'Vienna has melody'.

Viennese melodies once rang out
across the big pond,
and Uncle Sam from the U.S.A.
liked it straight away.
In return
he plays rhythms,
Vindobona listens
and then tells him
that sounds so nice,
How about it?
if you swap?

Chorus

Mitzi sits with Jonny
on a bench in the park,
arm in arm, mouth to mouth
and it gets dark and strong.
Mitzi sings something, Jonny whistles something,
soon you hear nothing more
and so in beautiful Vienna
the tourist trade awakens.

Chorus

■ This song is part of a series exploring musical cultures from across the Atlantic. The music was composed by Fredy Salten, a pianist, conductor, and composer who worked in both the Netherlands and Great Britain. Salten was an accompanist for many choirs and artists, including the Viennese performer Cilly Wang and *Theater Pleasure,* led by Toon Hermans. The lyrics were written by journalist, author, and radio host Gerrit Hartog, known by his pseudonym 'Bob' Wallagh (1907–1967) . Wallagh was a versatile writer who also published under the name Gerard van den Amstel. His works include *Nacht over Nederland 1940-1945: Journalistieke reportage van vijf bezettingsjaren* (*Night over the Netherlands: Journalistic Reports of Five Years of Occupation,* co-authored with Marcus Jan Adriani Engels, 1945). The cover humorously contrasts a woman holding a potted plant and garden trowel with lively dancers and musicians around her. The bright yellow background and cartoonish figures evoke postwar swing culture's vibrancy and energy. The woman's bewildered expression suggests feeling out of place amid the exuberant swing craze. This playful illustration reflects the tension between tradition and modern dance trends in 1940s Dutch society.

Ik kan niet swingen, cover (1945)

IK KAN NIET SWINGEN!

Music: Fredy Salten / *Lyrics*: Bob Wallagh
Year of publication: 1946

Ik heb in mijn leventje consequent pech,
je wordt op den duur fataliste.
O, niet in mijn werk want ik heb
op kantoor een voortreff'lijke baan als typiste,
maar als ik eens uitga
in mijn vrije tijd
en ik maak bij een boy goede kansen,
dan raak ik constant mijn illusies weer kwijt
en dat komt moet U weten
door 't dansen.

Refrein
'k kom uit heel gegoede kringen,
'k kweek exotische seringen.
Ik zit vol betoveringen,
maar helaas, ik kan niet swingen.
Ik kan zwemmen, roeien, zingen,
'k maak het zwaantje aan de ringen,
ik doe honderd and're dingen,
maar, nou ja, maar, nou ja,
ik kan niet swingen.

Vorig jaar maakt' ik kennis met een Canadees,
Ik ging met hem uit voor'n verzetje
Hij zei: 'Let's have a dance',
maar het werd 'quite a case'
helaas alles behalv' een pretje…

Want hij slingerd' en zwaaide
me heen en terug
en ik wist me geen raad
met mijn beenen:

’t beviel mij maar half en
al gauw werd hij stug…
na ’n kwartier was de lieverd verdwenen…

Refrein

Ga ’k soms naar een dancing
met ’n heerlijke band,
dan begin ik van vreugde te stralen!
Dan voel ik me even
door ’t leven verwend,
als ze mij voor een foxtrotje halen,
maar zoodra hoor ik
zoo’n hartverscheurende
kreet ‘Swing it boys’
door de danszaal heen bleren,
of ’t duurt nog maar even en
voor je het weet,
zit ’k opnieuw midden
in de misère…

Refrein

Toch verlies ik de moed niet
want ik weet één ding,
zoo iets is toch niet blijvend
op aarde.
En je bouwt toch geen liefde
op ’n mode in swing.
een hart zoekt naar diepere waarden,
misschien staat er plots’ling
een boy voor m’n neus,
die zich uitslooft
in duizenden dingen
maar die eerlijk bekent:
Lieve schat, ’t spijt me heusch,

’k Heb je lief,
maar ’k heb maling aan swingen!

Refrein

I CANNOT SWING!

I consistently have bad luck in my little life,
you become fatalistic in the long run.
Oh, not in my work because I have
an excellent job as a typist at the office,
but when I go out
in my spare time
and I take a good chance with a boy,
I constantly lose my illusions
and the reason you should know
is dancing.

Chorus:
I come from high society,
I grow exotic lilacs.
I’m full of enchantments,
But alas, I cannot swing.
I can swim, row, sing,
I make the swan dip,
I do a hundred other things,
but, well, but, well,
I cannot swing.

Last year I made acquaintance with a Canadian,
I went out with him for some fun
He said, ‘Let’s have a dance’,
but it turned out to be quite a case
Unfortunately everything except fun...

Cause he was swingin’ and swingin’
me back and forth

And I didn't know what to do
with my legs:
it only half pleased me and
soon he got stiff....
after fifteen minutes the dear was gone....

Chorus

Sometimes I go to a dance
with a great band,
I start to beam with joy!
For a moment
spoiled by life,
when they take me for a foxtrot,
But soon I hear
such a heartbreaking
cry 'Swing it boys'
blaring through the dance hall,
or it'll just be a moment and
before you know it,
I'll be back
in the misery...

Chorus

Yet I don't lose heart
because I know one thing,
such a thing is not permanent
on earth.
And you don't build love
on a fashion in swing.
A heart searches for deeper values,
maybe suddenly
A boy in front of me
showing off
In a thousand things

But who honestly confesses:
Sweetheart, I'm really sorry,
I love you,
But I don't care for swinging!

Chorus

■ Louis Noiret (1896–1968) was a Dutch pianist, singer, arranger, author, and composer who adopted the French version of his German surname, Schwarz. He began his career as a pianist with Jan-Louis Pisuisse's renowned cabaret company. Noiret frequently collaborated with Dutch poet H. Joosten, including on the *Hymn for Europe* in 1948. The cover expresses gratitude to the United States for its role in liberating Europe during World War II. Uncle Sam, symbolizing America, dances with a Dutch girl in traditional attire, holding tulips—a national Dutch symbol. Their matching red, white, and blue stripes emphasize shared values of freedom and unity. The background, featuring tulip fields, a windmill, and modern American skyscrapers, highlights cultural exchange and postwar optimism.

America, We Thank You, cover (1949)

AMERICA, WE THANK YOU

Music: Louis Noiret / *Lyrics*: G. Bon and H. Joosten
Year of publication: ca. 1949

Schepen komen binnen en een nieuwe toekomst daagt.
Nederland herstelt zich door de Marshall hulp geschraagd.
Het wil vol vertrouwen, moedig, onversaagd,
Sjouwen,... Bouwen...
Hoort hoe hier het lied van d'arbeid tot bezinnen dringt.
Ziet hoe Hollands kracht hier ieder mens tot werken dwingt,
Luister naar ons Volk dat toch zo gaarne zingt:
Vrijheid,... Blijheid...

Refrein:
America, We Thank You!
Je hebt veel goeds gedaan.
Wij kunnen dank zij Marshall nog op eigen benen staan.
Wij klagen niet, versagen niet,
wij vragen slechts spontaan:
Oh Gee! Good old America
Geef Holland toch 'Vrij baan!'

Heus, wij weten en vergeten nooit dat er een plicht,
Op een straks weer levend en volwaardig Holland ligt.
Want al is Uw streven op één doel gericht:
Leven,... Geven...
Al de nu geboden hulp die ons weer sterkt en staalt,
Moet door onze arbeid toch terug worden betaald.
Kunnen wij dit niet, dan is ons lot bepaald:
Dreigend,... Zwijgend...

Refrein

Nederland is niet zo groot, maar 't telt toch altijd mee
Daar het veel presteerde in z'n landen overzee
Voorspoed en vooruitgang, welvaart, rust en vree,
Kwamen,... Samen...

Kwade machten trachten thans gesteund door macht en geld
Ons vandaar te drijven, met veel list en door geweld
Mocht hen dit gelukken, zijn we 'uitgeteld'
Smaad'lijk,... Schaad'lijk...

Refrein

Ieder roept om vrede en verlangt naar veiligheid
Niemand wil meer oorlog of wenst weer 'n broederstrijd
Toch heerst er geen éénheid, ieder gaat z'n weg,
Jagend,... Klagend...

Naastenliefde is een leus, doch zonder fundament,
Als de mens op aard z'n Christenplichten niet meer kent.
Ieder moet beginnen: bij zichzelf het eerst
Waarheid,... Klaarheid...

Refrein

AMERICA, WE THANK YOU

Ships come in and a new future dawns.
Holland recovers underpinned by Marshall aid.
It drives confidently, boldly, undaunted,
Lugging, ... Building...
Hear how here the song of labor urges reflection.
See how Holland's strength forces every man to work,
Listen to our people who still love to sing:
Freedom, ... happiness....

Chorus:
America, We Thank You!
You've done a lot of good.
We can stand on our own two feet thanks to Marshall.
We do not complain, we do not fade,
we merely ask spontaneously:
Oh Gee! Good old America
Give Holland a free ride!

Truly, we know and never forget that there lies a duty,
On a soon living and fully-fledged Holland.
For though you aim for one goal:
Living,... Giving....
All the help now offered that strengthens and steels us again,
Must be repaid by our labor.
If we cannot, our fate is determined:
Threatening, ... Silent....

Chorus

Holland isn't that big, but it always counts
Since it achieved much in its overseas countries
Prosperity and progress, wealth, peace and joy,
Came... Together...

Evil powers now supported by power and money seek
To drive us from there, with much cunning and by force
Should they succeed, we're 'counted out'.
Disgraceful,... Harmful....

Chorus

Everyone calls for peace and longs for safety
No one wants war or brotherly battle again
Yet there is no unity, each goes his way,
Chasing, ... Complaining...

Charity is a motto, yet without foundation,
When mankind on earth no longer knows its Christian duties.
Each must begin: with himself first
Truth,... Clarity....

Chorus

■ Barend Renden composed a number of religious cantatas, with titles in Dutch, English, and German, such as *De strijd volbracht*, *God in den hoog' alleen*, *Paascantate*, *Steal Away*, *Were You There*, *Du bist's dem Ruhm und Ehre*, *Groot zijn de werken des Heren*, *Nobody Knows*, and *My Lord, What A Morning.* His *Bevrijdingslied 1945,* dedicated to the mayor of Utrecht, Ter Pelkwijk, was written between May 7 and 10, 1945. The cover celebrates the Netherlands' liberation at the end of World War II. A bold red flag, symbolizing freedom and resilience, dominates the design. The dedication to Mayor Ter Pelkwijk highlights civic pride and the return to normalcy.

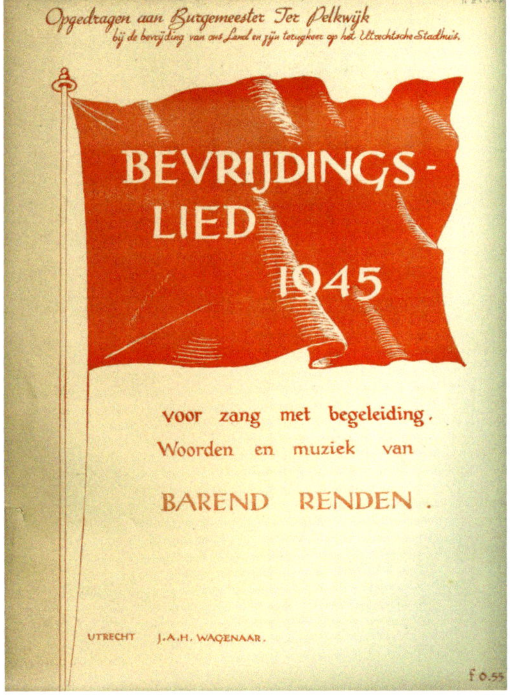

Bevrijdingslied, cover (1945)

BEVRIJDINGSLIED 1945

Music and lyrics: Barend Renden
Year of publication: 1945

Ons Nederland, ons Vaderland is vrij, is vrij!
Oranjehuis en Nederland weer zij aan zij.
De tirannie, de wreedheid moest wijken voor het recht,
Na alle leed kwam zege, wij zijn niet meer geknecht!
Nu mogen wij weer juichen en jublen blij,
Ons mooie, dierb're Vaderland is vrij, is vrij!

Weer wappert onze fiere vlag, ons rood, wit, blauw,
Symbool van strijd en zegepraal maar ook van trouw,
Hoe klopt ons hart van vreugde, hoe dankbaar zijn wij God,
Dat Hij ons lieve Vaderland bespaarde 't schrik'lijkst lot.
Omhoog nu onze vrije vlag, ons rood, wit, blauw,
O kleuren van ons Nederland, wij zijn U trouw!

LIBERATION SONG 1945

Our Netherlands, our Fatherland is free, is free!
The House of Orange and Holland once again side by side.
Tyranny, cruelty had to give way to justice,
After all the suffering came victory, we are enslaved no more!
Now we may cheer and rejoice again,
Our lovely, dear Fatherland is free, is free!

Once again our proud flag flies, our red, white, and blue,
Symbol of battle and triumph as well as loyalty,
How our hearts beat with joy, how grateful we are to God,
That He spared our dear homeland the most terrible fate.
Up now our free flag, our red, white, and blue,
Oh colors of our Netherlands, we are true to Thee!

Peter Lindeman and Piet van der Schaar collaborated on several patriotic and political songs, including *Amsterdam*, *Holland*, and *Pro Libertate*. Their song *Peace to All* is dedicated to displaced persons—those forced to remain abroad and unable to return home on their own, such as prisoners of war, forced laborers, concentration camp survivors, and Eastern Europeans who fled the advancing Russian army. In 1944, the Allies estimated that there were 11.3 million displaced persons. Lindeman's body of work was diverse, spanning from songs and choral pieces like *Jubilee Hymn 1914* and *Een roep gaat over de aarde. Vrede voor Vietnam 1966-1971*, to compositions for organ and piano, as well as books on music theory. *Peace to All* was published by G. Alsbach & Co. in Amsterdam. The cover features a powerful symbol of postwar peace and unity. A dove, universally representing peace, soars above a globe wrapped in a musical staff with the title text, linking music to harmony and reconciliation. Below, a handshake between two differently shaded hands emphasizes themes of racial and global solidarity. The soft, cloud-like background suggests hope and a brighter future. Created with elegant typography, it promotes peace through music and cooperation across divides.

Vrede voor allen, cover (1945)

VREDE VOOR ALLEN

Music and lyrics: Peter Lindeman
Year of publication: 1945

Mensen van de grote aarde
sluit U aan, verenigt U,
eenheid heeft de grootste waarde
voor de vrede, doet het nu.
Vrede, vrede, vrede voor allen.

Wilt toch allen samen strijden
voor de vrede op deez' aard.
Laat U door de liefde leiden
samen één, komt weest paraat.
Vrede, vrede, vrede voor allen.

Goede mensen, wilt toch horen,
nog is 't tijd, bezint U goed:
Laat de vrede niet verstoren,
brengt de vrijheid, waar het moet.
Vrede, vrede, vrede voor allen.

Komt dan mensen nu tezamen,
sluit U aan en doet een daad,
laat ons saam een plan beramen,
dat voorkomt het grootste kwaad.
Vrede, vrede, vrede voor allen.
Ieder wil in vrede leven
't is een recht, verstaat het wel;
Laat de vrede ons gegeven,
niet ontaarden in een hel.
Vrede, vrede, vrede voor allen.

Moet de mens dan altijd lijden
door't geweld op deze aard?
Neen, wij zullen samen strijden

voor het einde van het zwaard.
Vrede, vrede, vrede voor allen.

Komt nu mensen aangetreden!
Gordt U allen tot de strijd,
vecht verbeten voor de vrede,
doet een daad en weest bereid.
Vrede, vrede, vrede voor allen.

Na een macht van 't diepste duister
komt toch eenmaal 't Grote Licht,
dat dan straalt met heerlijk luister,
over 't rijk door God gesticht.
Vrede, vrede, vrede voor allen.

PEACE TO ALL

People of the great earth
Join, unite,
Unity has the greatest value
For peace, do it now.
Peace, peace, peace to all.

Will you all strive together
For peace on this earth.
Be guided by love
Together as one, come forth.
Peace, peace, peace to all.
Good people, please listen,
There is still time, consider well:
Let peace not be disturbed,
Bring freedom where it is due.
Peace, peace, peace to all.

Come now, people,
Join together and do an act,
Let us join together in a plan

that will prevent the greatest evil.
Peace, peace, peace to all.

Everyone wants to live in peace
It's a right, understand it well;
Let the peace given to us
not degenerate into hell.
Peace, peace, peace to all.

Must man then always suffer
By violence on this earth?
No, we shall fight together
for the end of the sword.
Peace, peace, peace to all.

Come now people!
Consecrate yourselves to battle,
Fight doggedly for peace,
Do a deed and be ready.
Peace, peace, peace to all.

After a power of deepest darkness
Yet once will come the Great Light
Which will shine with glorious splendor
over the kingdom founded by God.
Peace, peace, peace to all.

■ *Het vrije Nederland. Bevrijdingslied 1940-1945* was originally composed for brass band, but in 1945, pianist Annie Sluijter-Hoogenboom arranged it for piano. The composer, Johan Sluijter, had already made his mark in 1932 by publishing a collection of Dutch popular songs in collaboration with Leopold Weniger, titled *Zoo zingt Holland: Potpourri over populaire volks- en soldatenliederen* (This is How Holland Sings: Potpourri of Popular Folk and Soldiers' Songs). The cover symbolizes Dutch resilience and triumph during World War II. The central figure, a roaring lion—the enduring emblem of Dutch strength and freedom—breaks free from chains, representing liberation from Nazi occupation. Radiating golden rays symbolize hope, victory, and a brighter future. Bold red, white, and blue colors reflect the Dutch national identity. The powerful imagery and dynamic typography embody the nation's pride, strength, and the celebratory spirit of liberation.

Het vrije Nederland. Bevrijdingslied 1940-1945, cover (1945)

HET VRIJE NEDERLAND. BEVRIJDINGSLIED 1940–1945

Music: Johan Sluijter / *Lyrics*: Herre de Vos
Year of publication: 1945

Zie, daar waaien onze wimpels weer
En de fiere vlaggen wapp'ren!
Nog kreeg men Holland niet terneer
Het oude volk der dapp'ren!
Na jaren vol van zwart verdriet
Van verdrukking, haat en schand,
Weer klinkt opeens een jubellied,
Langs bosch en duin en strand:

Refrein
Omdat wij weer vrije burgers zijn,
Van het vrije Nederland!
Omdat wij weer vrije burgers zijn,
Van het vrije Nederland!

Een bevrijdingszucht welt uit ons hart,
Want vervuld zijn onze wenschen:
Geleden is die bitt're smart,
Wij leven weer als menschen!
Een vreugde, die ten hart uit dringt,
Vindt nu weer klank door heel 't land
Komt jubelt, juicht en danst en zingt
En springt eens uit den band:

Refrein

Nu des vijands listen zijn gestrand
Sla de handen uit de mouwen;
Kom, dienen wij het Vaderland
Als Willem van Nassaue.
De vrijheid lacht als zonneschijn
Elken toeleg weer te schand.

Laat uit het nu met tweedracht zijn
En reikt elkaar de hand:

Refrein

FREE HOLLAND. LIBERATION SONG 1940 1945

Behold, there our pennants blow again
And the proud flags fly!
Still Holland was not brought down
The ancient people of the brave!
After years of black sorrow
Of oppression, hatred and shame,
Again suddenly a song of jubilation sounds
Along woods and dunes and beaches

Chorus:
Because we are free citizens again
Of the free Netherlands!
Because we are free citizens again
Of the free Netherlands!

A sigh of relief wells up from our hearts,
Because our wishes are fulfilled:
Gone is that bitter grief
We live like human beings again!
A joy that pierces our hearts
Now resounds throughout the land
Come and rejoice and dance and sing
And for once break loose

Chorus

Now that the enemy's tricks have failed
Roll up our sleeves
Come, let's serve the Fatherland
As William of Nassau.

Freedom smiles like sunshine
Each conspiracy is put to shame
Let discord be over now
And reach out to one another

Chorus

■ Albert de Booy (born Arthur Charles Albert de Booij on November 27, 1897, in Oud-Vroenhoven, Limburg; died May 2, 1971, in Rotterdam) was a composer and arranger active during and after WWII. He made recordings with orchestras like The Ramblers, including the piece *Korenbloemenblauw* (recorded in Hilversum, Hof van Holland, on April 4, 1939). Among his other musical works are *Dat moet je niet doen Amalia, Mijn tante Alida speelt mondharmonika,* and *Trees heeft een Canadees.* In May 1923, he married Roosje van der Klein, and the couple had four daughters. The cover reflects post-World War II liberation themes, depicting a playful interaction between a flirtatious Canadian soldier and a Dutch woman. The soldier symbolizes Allied liberators, warmly welcomed after ending Nazi occupation. The army jeep reinforces the military presence, while the romanticized, humorous tone highlights joy and cultural exchange in postwar Europe. Promoting the song as a 'Succesnummer', the illustration captures the optimism, relationships, and lighthearted entertainment that emerged in the aftermath of liberation.

Trees heeft een Canadees, cover (1945)

Trees heeft een Canadees

Music: Albert de Booy / *Lyrics*: Lou de Groot
Year of publication: 1945

In mijn straatje woont een meisje
Luist'rend naar de naam van Trees
'n Echte Hollandse verschijning
Knap, en aardig in d'r vlees
Nooit moest zij iets van verkering
Vrijen vond ze ongezond
Maar direct na de bevrijding
Ging 't gerucht van mond tot mond.

Refrein:
Trees heeft een Canadees
O, wat is dat kindje in d'r sas
Trees heeft een Canadees
Samen in de jeep en dan vol gas
Al vindt zij dat Engels lang niet mis is
Wil zij dolgraag weten wat een kiss is
Trees heeft een Canadees
O, wat is dat kindje in d'r sas.

Sprak een Hollandse aanbidder
Haar van trouwen of zoiets
Kreeg hij dadelijk ten antwoord
'Niks ervan, ik koop een fiets!'
Nu is Treesje aan 't studeren
Iedere middag neemt zij les
Want tot nu toe was haar Engels
Enkel maar: 'Oke en yes!'

Refrein

Als ze maar een uniform ziet
Raakt ze hevig van de wijs

Vraag je haar: 'Weet je wat "love" is?'
Zegt ze smachtend: 'Very nice!'
Och, hoe zal het gaan met Treesje
Als haar boy uit Canada
Binnenkort weer zal verdwijnen
Naar zijn 'home' in Ottawa.

Refrein

TREES HAS GOT A CANADIAN

A girl lives in my street
She goes by the name of Trees
A real Dutch appearance
Good looking and plump
She didn't need to be courted
She considered it healthy to make love
But right after the liberation
The rumors were going around.

Chorus:
Trees has got a Canadian
Oh, how smitten the child is
Trees has got a Canadian
Together in the jeep and then full throttle
Though she thinks English isn't half bad
She really wants to know what a 'kiss is
Trees has got a Canadian
Oh, how smitten the child is.

When a Dutch admirer spoke
To her of marriage and such
The answer he got was
"Nothing doing (absolutely not), I'll buy a bike!"
Now Treesje is studying
Every afternoon she has a lesson
Till now the extent of her English

Was only: “Okay” and “yes!”

Chorus

When she sees a uniform
She goes out of her mind
You ask her “Do you know what love is?”
She says wistfully: “Very nice!”
Oh, what will happen to Treesje
If her boy from Canada
Disappears before long
To his “home” in Ottawa

Chorus

POSTLUDE: SONGS OF LIBERATION WITH THE CANADIAN TULIP FESTIVAL

Jo Riding

Since 1953, the Canadian Tulip Festival has stood as a powerful symbol of the enduring friendship between Canada and the Netherlands. This bond was born out of the gratitude expressed by the Dutch people for Canada's pivotal role in the liberation of the Netherlands during the Second World War.

Each year, our festival celebrates the renewal of spring and commemorates a unique royal and military story deeply rooted in Ottawa's history. The tradition began in 1945 when then-Princess Juliana gifted the city 100,000 tulip bulbs upon her return to the Netherlands after spending her country's Nazi occupation in the safety of Canada's capital during the war. Then-Princess Juliana gave birth to her third daughter Princess Margriet at the Ottawa Civic Hospital which is only blocks away from our Festival site. The Netherlands has continued the tradition, giving at least 10,000 tulip bulbs annually to Ottawa for the last 80 years.

The 69th Edition of the Festival faced unprecedented challenges posed by the COVID-19 pandemic in 2020, which could have easily disrupted the festival's celebrations. Instead, a timely and fortuitous collaboration with Prof. Dr. Frank Mehring, esteemed scholar in American Studies at

Radboud University in the Netherlands, helped us find an innovative way to maintain the festival's spirit and connect with a global audience through a video series entitled *Songs of Liberation*.

This cross-Atlantic collaboration seamlessly connected the festival's historical significance with contemporary reflections on freedom and solidarity through the universal language of music.

Prof. Mehring curated eleven *Songs of Liberation* videos, offering thoughtful insights into the themes of liberation and celebration. Now, the *Songs of Liberation* series has become an integral part of the Canadian Tulip Festival, enriching the experience for attendees by creating meaningful moments of contemplation and celebration.

One of the most touching moments I witnessed at the Festival was seeing three older couples stop everything and dance with each other on our Great Lawn once they heard the opening strains of Lili Marlene drifting from our Main Stage. While they swirled and danced they sang the song to each other, knowing every word. What was perhaps even more affecting was watching all the younger generations step back, creating an impromptu dancefloor on the grass amongst our tulip gardens. The audience was entranced and I believe we all saw ourselves in this youthful display of popular culture and custom from another time.

Liberation songs, whether sung during wartime or in the years that followed, have an enduring appeal because they embody universal themes. They evoke the struggles of the past, yet remain profoundly relevant to the challenges of the present.

Another example of this bridge to modern relevance is Vera Lynn's timeless classic, "We'll Meet Again." We adopted this song as our unofficial Festival Anthem in 2019, and not long after Queen Elizabeth II used that song in her 2020 address regarding the pandemic and the resulting lockdowns. She urged us to look to the resilience of the past to navigate the challenges of the present, making the song an emotional touchstone during a time of isolation and uncertainty. After the speech, this song became more poignant and relevant in the public gaze than it had been in quite a few years, and web searches for Vera Lynn increased across the world, and she was brought back to centre stage. This resurgence of interest in Lynn's music underscores how liberation songs can resonate across eras, offering comfort and connection in difficult times.

By showcasing the *Songs of Liberation* series on our Main Stage each year, the Canadian Tulip Festival honors the sacrifices and triumphs of those touched by war. These performances inspire new generations to reflect on the enduring power of hope and solidarity. Through this music, we celebrate not only our shared history but also the continued partnership between Canada and the Netherlands.

The *Songs of Liberation* series and this very book itself play a vital role in preserving and sharing these connections. They ensure that the legacy of courage, gratitude, and unity remains alive for future generations, deepening our appreciation for the ties that bind us across an ocean, and an ocean of time.

ACKNOWLEDGMENTS

Books are born of ideas, but they grow thanks to people—this one is no exception. This book exists thanks to the insights, generosity, guidance, and inspiration of many remarkable contributors, collaborators, and friends. Bringing the liberation soundtrack to life would have been impossible without Jens Barnieck, a concert pianist and close friend who played a crucial role in researching and performing the liberation songs from the border region of the Netherlands and Germany. I am particularly grateful for the support and cooperation of Wiel Lenders and Rense Havinga from the Freedom Museum (formerly National Liberation Museum 1944-45) in Groesbeek.

Special thanks go to Anja Adriaans, who was the heart and soul of many liberation-themed projects. I also extend my gratitude to the staff of the Department of American Studies at Radboud University for their endeavors. This book was created in conjunction with a series of concerts in Nijmegen, Groesbeek, and Kleve, where schoolchildren from Karel de Grote College in Nijmegen, Joseph Beuys Gesamtschule (formerly Ganztagsrealschule Hoffmannallee) in Kleve, dancers from Tanzschule Seidl, and solo singers Saskia Bak, Tom van den Heuvel, and Sarah Konig performed many of the songs covered in these pages. My thanks also go to Jutta Biesemann for her confidence in me and her coordination of the preparations in Kleve. I owe a debt of gratitude to all of them for their dedication, expertise, and enthusiasm.

I also thank the following institutions and organizations that supported the performances of the Liberation Songs in the fall of 2014: Vfonds – National Fund for Peace, Freedom and Veterans, Liberation Route Europe, the Freedom Museum, Rhine–Waal Euroregion, the Joseph Beuys Gesamtschule Kleve, and the Radboud Institute of Culture and History, and particularly my colleagues from the research group Cultures of War and Liberation, for their support and advice.

I am deeply grateful to the many people who contributed to making the concert and this book possible. My thanks go to Britt de Bakker, Hans Bak, Petra Bay, Diana Beermann, Jutta Biesemann, Monika Lohmann, Claudia Rehder, Joost Rosendaal, Wilfried Röth, Marco Rumler, and Ludger Seidl. Additionally, I thank the singers and dancers from the schools in the border area of the Netherlands and Germany. Without their voices and dances, the soundtrack of liberation would have remained hidden away in archive boxes. Through their performances, these young artists now remind us of the sacrifices made and the true price of freedom. My heartfelt thanks to Nina Balk, Tobias Bonk, Ronja Brandenburg, Alina Dautwitz, Lara Dautwitz, Ate van Delden, Nikia Demir, editor Eddy Determeyer of Dr. Jazz Magazine, Chantal Ewig, Lea Friedl, Jana Grabinski, Jana Groenewald, Sophia Hövelmann, Isabel Liebrand, Johanna Liebrand, Yvonne Liffers, Michelle Look, Shari Müller, Marike Oversteegen, Lisa Papenguth, Mina Perez, Richard Piepenbrock, Lilav Schahin, Helena Thomsen, Laura van den Berg, Milena Vehreschild, Annika Vijselaar, Pia Weidemann, Michelle Wildenbeest, and Valeria Wolfert. I would like to express my gratitude to Grant Hooker, Jo Riding, and their team for their dedicated efforts in presenting the liberation songs at the 2020 Canadian Tulip Festival.

Above all, I am deeply grateful to my dear colleague and friend, Hugo Keesing, whose unwavering dedication and generosity made this book possible. From our very first meeting in the Dutch city of Ede in 2013, Hugo's guidance, support, and generosity in sharing his extensive knowledge have been a continual source of inspiration. His fascinating collection of sheet music has been indispensable, and without it, there would be no *Soundtrack of Liberation*.

Hugo, this book is for you! Your dedication to preserving and sharing musical history has profoundly shaped my work. Thank you for being an exceptional mentor and friend.

NOTES

1 I would like to thank the following persons for their support in tracing the sheet music, photos, and for their inspiring suggestions: Rense Havinga from the Freedom Museum , Groesbeek, American collector of Dutch WWII sheet music Hugo Keesing, Anja Adriaans, and pianist Jens Barnieck for helping to make the music resound again.

2 See Benjamin Filene. *Romancing the Folk: Public Memory & American Roots Music.* Chapel Hill: University of North Carolina Press, 2000: 198.

3 The function of music as an expression of protest and the struggle for freedom has been analyzed in a variety of ways among scholars. See e.g. Christopher Flannery-McCoy, 'Analysis and History of Major Choral Arrangements of "We Shall Overcome".' *We Shall Overcome. Essays on a Great American Song.* Ed. Victor V. Bobetsky. Lanham, Boulder, New York, London: Rowman & Littlefield, 2015: 59–76; Samuel Floyed, *The Power of Black Music: Interpreting its History from Africa to the United States.* New York: Oxford UP, 1995; Michael J. Gilmour, *The Gospel According to Bob Dylan. The Old, Old Story for Modern Times.* Louisville: Westminster John Knox Press, 2011; Brian Ward, 'Sounds and Silences: Music and the March on Washington.' *Staging a Dream: Untold Stories and Transatlantic Legacies of the March on Washington.* Ed. Britta Waldschmidt-Nelson, Marcia Chatelain, and Sharon Monteith. Bulletin of the German Historical Institute 11 (2015): 25–48; Frank Mehring, '"Only a Pawn in their Game?" Civil Rights Sounding Signatures in the Summer of 1963.' *Sonic Politics: Music and Social Movements in the Americas.* Olaf Kaltmeier and Wilfried Raussert (eds.). New York: Routledge, 2019 (51-72).

4 The intermedial work of Pussy Riot and the power of music to intervene in contemporary political debates and reshape historical moments are currently showcased in the exhibition 'Velvet Terrorism: Pussy Riot's Russia' at Haus der Kunst. Through a combination of videos, photographs, and texts, the exhibition captures the intensifying conflict between the feminist collective and state authorities, culminating in Russia's invasion of Ukraine. By challenging conventional curatorial practices, the exhibition provides a dense, immersive experience. See https://www.hausderkunst.de/eintauchen/velvet-terrorism-pussy-riots-russia

5 This particular sequence is featured in the trailer for the film.

6 Unless otherwise noted, translations of Dutch song lyrics are primarily rendered as literal interpretations to preserve the fidelity of the original text. However, where cultural nuances, idiomatic expressions, or contextual elements require alternative phrasing for clarity or resonance in English, such adjustments are clearly marked and explained.

7 The concert program, Music from the Countries of Our Liberators, honored the nations that played key roles in World War II liberation— the United States, Great Britain, Canada, and Poland. The repertoire included two movements from Dean Burry's *Tracing Colville*, Witold

Lutosławski's *Little Suite*, Sir Edward Elgar's *Sea Pictures*, Opus 37, and Charles Ives' *Variations on America*. Held on September 21, 2024 in Nijmegen, the event celebrated the cultural and historical contributions of these allied nations through their music.

8 Parts of this text appeared earlier under the title 'Liberation Songs: Music and the Cultural Memory of the Dutch Summer of 1945' in the anthology *Politics and Cultures of Liberation: Media, Memory, and Projections of Democracy* (Brill: Leiden, Boston, 2018): 149-176. The current text is an updated and expanded version of *Soundtrack van de Bevrijding. Swingen, Zingen en Dansen op Weg naar Vrijheid* (Nijmegen: Vantilt, 2015).

9 In the case of this image, ruins are carefully kept outside of the photographic frame. The building we see is intact while the area behind where the photographer stands has been destroyed in an allegedly mistaken bombing by U.S. forces in February 1944.

10 See Wilfried Raussert and James Miller Jones *Travelling Sounds. Music, Migration, and Identity in the U.S. and Beyond*, 8.

11 In addition to Raussert and Jones's *Travelling Sounds,* see also Wagnleitner *Coca-Colonization and the Cold War*, which traces forms of Americanization and self-Americanization putting music and radio in correspondence with advertising, comics, literature, education, theater, and fashion. Alfred Hornung and Rüdiger Kunow suggested that in the field of literature a shift of attention away from representations of the global towards what they call 'culturally informed imaginings (...) of its effects' (197) might offer new insights into transnational networking, cultural mobility, and diaspora. This approach can also be made useful for understanding the soundtrack of liberation.

12 Jacques Attali, *Noise: The Political Economy of Music*, 4.

13 See William Uricchio, William. Things to Come in the American Studies–Media Studies Relationship. In: *American Studies Today. New Research Agendas*. Eds. Winfried Fluck, Erik Redling, Sabine Sielke, Hubert Zapf. Heidelberg: Universitätsverlag Winter, 2014 (363–382).

14 See Jay David Bolter and Richard Grusin. *Remediation. Understanding New Media*. Cambridge, MA: MIT Press, 2000.

15 Quoted in Kathleen E.R. Smith, *God Bless America: Tin Pan Alley Goes to War*. Lexington: UP of Kentucky, 2003: 74.

16 I have examined the cultural dimension and 'soft power' of the Marshall Plan in a variety of ways. See e.g. Frank Mehring, 'The Promises of "Young Europe": Cultural Diplomacy, Cosmopolitanism, and Youth Culture in the Films of the Marshall Plan.' *Journal of European American Studies*, Rob Kroes and Jean Kempf (eds.). 7.2 (2012). http://ejas.revues.org/9701

17 R. Murray Schafer, *The Thinking Ear: Complete Writings on Music Education*, 95.

18 The rise of sound studies has begun to make a significant impact on the humanities, as evidenced by recent anthologies like Jonathan Sterne's *Sound Studies Reader* (Routledge, 2012), which builds on his earlier landmark work, *The Audible Past: Cultural Origins of Sound Reproduction* (Durham: Duke UP, 2003). In Germany, Gerhard Paul and Ralph Schock's comprehensive handbook, *Der Sound des Jahrhunderts: Geräusche, Töne, Stimmen 1889 bis heute* (Bonn: BPB, 2013), further highlights this shift. Scholars are now rethinking the nature of sound, the act of listening, the role of music in modern life, and its interaction with the arts across transnational and transcultural contexts.

19 Quoted in Schafer, 94.

20 Hugo Keesing. *Youth in Transition: A Content Analysis of Two Decades of Popular Music*. Diss. Adelphi University, 1972: 2.

21 See Hugo Keesing's chapter in this book.
22 Hugo Keesing, retired adjunct associate professor of Psychology and American Studies at the University of Maryland, donated his collection of Dutch sheet music, which dealt in some form or another with the experience of liberation. Keesing was born in The Hague in 1951 and emigrated with his parents to the U.S. He had been interested in the political function of music during the Vietnam War as well as World War II. His Dutch sheet music collection of almost 300 songs provides a unique perspective on the soundtrack of liberation combining elaborate cover designs, musical scores and in many cases multilingual lyrics. Astonishingly, only a few of the songs are familiar to Dutch audiences apart from exceptions such as *Trees heeft een Canadees* or *Lili Marleen*. This is a curious surprise, which demands explanation.
23 From May 2 to September 30, 2007, the Resistance Museum (*Verzetsmuseum*) in Amsterdam offered an exhibition called 'Bevrijdingsmuziek', featuring a selection of covers and scores from 1944 and 1945.
24 I am grateful for Jens Barnieck tracing these biblical roots of liberation songs.
25 Jacques Attalie, *Noise: The Political Economy of Music*. Translated by Brian Massumi. Minneapolis: University of Minnesota Press, 1985.19.
26 Quoted in Cooke 12.
27 Jean Mitry, *The Aesthetics and Psychology of the Cinema*. Bloomington: Indiana University Press, 1997: 162
28 Winfried Fluck, *Romance with America? Essays on Culture, Literature, and American Studies*. Laura Bieger and Johannes Voelz (eds.). Heidelberg: Universitätsverlag Winter, 2009: 244.
29 Aline Sierp argues that since the 1990s the 'common experience of repression, dictatorship and genocide (...) turned into a point of reference for the definition of the [European] Union's values and political goals' (115). In the new millennium, new initiatives such as the Liberation Route Europe have tried to shift the focus away from the experience of trauma and destruction.
30 In addition to marching music, Nazis emphasized the importance of folk songs for ideological purposes. See for example Thomas Phleps, 'Musik und Ideologie' (2002).
31 As Gerard Groenveld explains in *Zo zong de NSB*, these songs have been forgotten over time (200).
32 See in this context Hanns-Werner Heister's entry on political music in *Die Musik in Geschichte und Gegenwart* (1997).
33 Interview with Rense Havinga conducted for the MA paper 'Liberation Songs' at Radboud University by Esther Adema, Litania de Graaf, and Rita Hynes in June 2014.
34 Annelies Jacobs and Karin Bijsterveld speak in this context of 'politics of sound' based on their analysis of Amsterdam diaries. See 'Der Klang der Besatzungszeit: Amsterdam 1940 bis 1945' (2013). See also Annelies Jacobs, *Het geluid van gisteren. Waarom Amsterdam vroeger ook niet stil was* (2014).
35 See Michael Gerhard Kaufman, *Orgel und Nationalsozialismus. Die ideologische Vereinnahmung des Instrumentes im 'Dritten Reich'* (1997).
36 Benedict Anderson, *Imagined Communities: Reflections on the Origin and Spread of Nationalism*, rev. ed. London: Verso, 2006: 7.
37 Walker Connor, *Ethnonationalism: The Quest for Understanding*. Princeton University Press, 1994: 93.
38 See Chapter 6, 'Sincerely Yours: The Trouble with Sentimentality and the Ban on Crooners', in Christina Baade's *Victory Though Harmony* (2012).

39 See in this context *Public Record Office: F.A. Voigt, PWE–Policy Meeting: Words and Phrases, Notes on Translation in BBC German Broadcasts*. Regarding the work of Carl Brinitzer, see in particular Conrad Puetter, 'Deutsche Emigranten und britische Propaganda' (1983).

40 Among many other songs, Herre de Vos also wrote the lyrics for the iconic liberation song *Het Vrije Nederland. Bevrijdingslied 1940–1945*.

41 Fitzroy MacLean, *Escape to Adventure*. Little, Brown & Co., 1950: 236.

42 The lyrics differ substantially in various publications of the song in the U.S. and Great Britain.

43 Next to Marlene Dietrich, Fred Astaire was among the best known American stars, who came to Maastricht in 1944. See Wim Klinkert's article 'Crossing Borders: Americans and the Liberation of the Netherlands' (565–578). According to Rense Havinga, Dietrich was in Maastricht in January 1945. The Freedom Liberation Museum has a guest book of the Hustinx family in which Dietrich left her signature on a 5-Franc bill.

44 The following part has been slightly modified based on the following article by the author: 'Rosies Across Ideologies: Intermedial and Transnational Approaches to an American Female Icon.' *Women and U.S. Politics. Historical and Contemporary Perspectives. Essays in Honor of Hans-Juergen Grabbe*. Julia Nitz and Axel R. Schaefer (eds.). Heidelberg: Winter Verlag, 2020 (103–124).

45 *Rosie the Riveter.* Words and Music by John Loeb and Redd Evans. New York: Paramount Music, 1942: 4.

46 Regarding the consequences of employers restoring the prewar sexual division of labor and the consequences for women's opportunities on the job market during the Cold War, see Rupp's analysis in 'From Rosie the Riveter to the global Assembly Line: American Women on the World Stage' (2004).

47 Transcription by Keesing.

48 Transcription by Keesing.

49 The cover explains that the song was featured by 'Phil Arden and the Douglas Bombardiers'.

50 They are included in the monograph *She Was on the Job: A Selection of World War 2 Songs about Rosies and Their 'Sisters.'* Hugo Keesing; Keesing Musical Archives, 2015.

51 Quoted in Eileen Southern, *The Music of Black Americans: A History.* 3rd ed. New York: Norton & Company, 1997: 347.

52 For further reference on the role of Bulterman in The Ramblers see *Jack Bulterman: The Ramblers Story* (1973) and Co de Kloet and Gabri de Wagt's *Mooi Holland? De Woelige Jaren van de Ramblers* (1981).

53 The Dutch original reads: 'Zij vroegen hem, van waar hij kwam: Hij zei: Jan Steenstraat Amsterdam.'

54 A reproduction of the photograph is featured in the first chapter of *Faces of Liberation*. Frank Mehring and Jaap Verheul (eds.). Amsterdam: Amsterdam University Press, 2025.

55 Rense Havinga in a personal email to the author, Sep. 24, 2024.

56 For an overview of the impact of international dances on Dutch culture, see Lutgard Mutsaers, *Beat Crazy* (1998). Mutsaers, however, starts with the role of dance in Dutch youth culture in the 1960s.

57 See Rense Havinga, 'De soundtrack van de bevrijding tentoonstellen.' *De Soundtrack van de Bevrijding*. Frank Mehring. Vantilt 2015: 102.

58 The original Dutch lyrics read: 'Daar komen de Canadezen, \ Ze kwamen van over d'oceaan, Ze waagden hun/bloed en hun leven, \Ze hebben in stormen van kogels gestaan, \Om ons weer de vrijheid te geven.

Waait vlaggen en wimpels nu hoog in de wind, \ Waar eind'lijk, God is geprezen, \ Verdrukking verplet wordt en vrijheid begint. \ En leve, leve de Canadezen!'

59 The song also offers a version with Dutch lyrics: 'Wie gaat er mee?/ Ik ga een straatje om./ Ik vind het tegenwoordig wel een leuke boel./ 't is geen: "Hou zee!" (daar lacht een ieder om)/ Maar 't is een/prettig en een sympathiek gevoel./ Wat een auto's suizen er doorlopend af en aan!/Wat een pittig en een zakelijk gedoe,/ Waar komt al dat mooie, reuze, vlugge spul vandaan?/ Waar gaan al die flinke knapen toch naar toe?/Ik fleur weer op, ik voel me heerlijk fit/ Omdat ik weet wat in die snelle wagens zit. / Kijk daar gaan de Knuks,/Al wat zij doen,/ Dat doen zij kwiek en fluks!/Voor die kwieke Knuks/Hebben ze kleine auto's voor twee stuks./ Voor hun moed en hun materiaal/ Gingen de moffen aan den haal/Kijk daar gaan Knuks,/ Al wat zij doen, dat doen zij kwiek en fluks!'.

60 See Havinga, 105 in the original Dutch version. See also Havinga's contribution to this book.

61 Havinga, 105.

62 See Havinga's contribution to this book.

63 Jan Hendriks, *Pianist in Bevrijdingstijd.* Nijmegen: Braekkenstein, 2004: 73. Translation by Hans Bak, 115.

64 For an excellent close reading of Birney's poem, see Hans Bak, 'On the Road to Nijmegen—Earle Birney and Alex Colville, 1944-1945.' In: *Politics and Cultures of Liberation. Media, Memory, and Projections of Democracy*. Brill: Leiden, Boston, 2018 (113-145): 118-120.

65 See Michiel Horn, 'More Than Cigarettes, Sex and Chocolate. The Canadian Army in the Netherlands, 1944-1945. In: *Journal of Canadian Studies / Revue des Études Canadiennes*, 16.3 (Fall 1981): 156–173.

66 Enne Koops provided a helpful overview of Dutch emigration to North America and traced the cultural elements of attraction between the liberation and Marshall aid. See *De Dynamiek van een Emigratiecultuur* (2010), in particular 104–139. The tone of the songs changed from humorously describing the romantic encounters between liberators and Dutch women towards warning and accusing the men from overseas (Havinga, 105).

67 See Horn, 'More Than Cigarettes, Sex and Chocolate': 170.

68 It is important to note that feelings of anger and jealousy were only short-lived. Rense Havinga explains: 'When the last allied soldiers left the Netherlands in the spring of 1946, the debate lost its venom and the Dutch public soon forgot about their own harsh treatment of the girls. The only ones who continued to suffer the scorn of society where the many single mothers raising a child in the postwar period. Public memories of the Allied soldiers became more positive again, and while memories of the perceived immorality of Dutch girls remained, they were surrounded by an air of nostalgia and romance. Of the many songs written about the relationships, only the very popular song 'Trees heeft een Canadees' endured in public memory. It is a song that has a few firm words of advice for the Dutch girls, but an overall quite positive tone. Songs like *Girl, watch what you do* and *The Canadian Fever* lost their appeal to an audience eager to romanticize the history of liberation.' Havinga, 108.

69 English words by Bart Ekkers.

70 Translation by F. Mehring.

71 The response to new American musical styles of African American origin remained controversial in many European countries. For example, despite initial efforts to dismiss African American music as primitive, immoral, and alien, the BBC shifted toward a more positive portrayal of jazz in 1943, recognizing its ability to lift spirits during wartime. Notably, with

the establishment of the American Forces Network in July 1943, this music became 'a catalyst for those worried about Americanization, which they regarded as a threat to the survival of a distinctly British culture' (*Victory Through Harmony*, 177). Even German radio propaganda exploited jazz to attract British and other Allied soldiers, inserting propaganda messages between the songs. Horst J.P. Bergmeier and Rainer E. Lotz provide a detailed account of Nazi subversive radio programming and Goebbels's propaganda orchestra, led by crooner Karl ('Charlie') Schwedler, in *Hitler's Airwaves: The Inside Story of Nazi Radio Broadcasting and Propaganda Swing* (1997).

72 See van de Leur, 'The Reception and Development of Jazz in the Netherlands,' 180.

73 Walter van de Leur traced the history and reception of jazz music in the Netherlands by looking at the Dutch magazine *Jazzwereld,* which was published between 1931 and 1940. He explained that '[t]he purpose of both *De Jazzwereld* and the Nederlandse Hot Club (NHC) was to promote and defend jazz, to educate players, listeners and adversaries alike, to organize concerts, competitions, and lectures, to push radio stations to play more jazz, and to establish a network of like-minded jazz lovers' (unpaginated).

74 One of the earliest historians who described the function of jazz in German culture was Horst H. Lange in his overview *Jazz in Deutschland. Die Deutsche Jazz-Chronik 1900–1966* (1966).

75 Here, I follow Bernd Polster's conclusion regarding the fine line between discrediting and condoning swing music in the 1930s and 40s. See *Swing Heil! Jazz im Nationalsozialismus* (1989).

76 The original Dutch reads: 'We mochten geen Amerikaanse nummers spelen. We speelden natuurlijk wel Amerikaanse nummers, maar dan werd de titel veranderd. Jazz met blues, dat werd *Mijn blauwe jas... Steeplechase* was *Hindernisrennen* en ga zo maar door.' Quoted in de Kloet and de Wagt, *Mooi Holland?*, 76.

77 However, the double meaning of the song was later brought to the attention of the *Reichskommissariat* when it was performed at concerts. In a letter dated September 25, 1943, Theo Udern Masman, leader of The Ramblers, was informed that *Morgen komt een nieuwe dag* should no longer be performed as it could provoke 'unwanted reactions' from the audience. See de Kloet and de Wagt, 81.

78 The original Dutch reads: 'Het Rijkscommissariaat deelt mede, dat U in Arnhem een concert gaf, dat erg naar Engelsche Jazz zweemde. Ook speelde U te veel Fransche nummers en slechts één enkel Duitsch. U moet *veel meer* Duitsche nummers gaan spelen, anders zullen we maatregelen nemen.' Quoted in de Kloet and de Wagt, 81.

79 Van de Leur explains that it took several years before Dutch audiences could see and hear American jazz stars such as Louis Armstrong, Sideny Bechet, Duke Ellington, Dizzy Gillespie, and others live on stage. 'The Reception and Development of Jazz in the Netherlands (1945-1970s)', 183.

80 The information on the hit tune of The Ramblers is quite sparse and mentioned only in passing in Bulterman's *The Ramblers Story* (1973) and Co de Kloet and Gabri de Wagt's *Mooi Holland? De Woelige Jaren van de Ramblers* (1981).

81 '*Bouncin' in Bavaria*, de van de AFN welbekende "tune", was een van de beste nummers van de avond,' 6 Feb. 1950, 7.

82 For a biographical overview, see Bulterman, *Ramblers Story*.

83 German jazz musician and teacher Carlo Bohländer explains that the German jazz scene benefitted immensely from the German drafting system at the outbreak of World War II. Since

many German jazz musicians were ordered to the frontlines, the positions in cafés, bars, and dance halls as well as radio stations had to be filled: 'The musicians came, above all, from occupied Belgium and Holland and generally demonstrated a higher jazz standard then their German counterparts' (170). In a similar vein, Horst Lange describes the Dutch swing orchestra lead by Ernst van 't Hoff as the most modern swing orchestra in Europe (139).

84 Wouters, 'Fear', 43.

85 See de Leur. The authors often fought an uphill battle against harsh attacks on jazz from the conservative press. Protestant critics urged the believers to resist the 'dangers of gymnastics'; Catholics such as the Bishop of Den Bosch, Monseigneur Diepen, warned that the 'modern pagan dances are an abyss of sin.' Others such as the magazine *De Muziek* described jazz as 'rubbish and a caricature of the modern orchestra.' The members of the socialist youth organization Arbeiders Jeugd Centrale saw in jazz a sign for the decay of civilization. For an overview of the negative responses to American jazz in the 1920s, see Wouters, 'Fear', 45-50.

86 Date of publication unknown. Considering the title with its reference to the liberation and the fact that the publication does not explicitly mention The Ramblers, we may infer that it might have been published between May 1945 and January 1946, when The Ramblers were banned in the Netherlands. The same title was later chosen for the book *The Ramblers Story: 38 Jaar, Máárrr... Wij Komen Terug* by Jack Bulterman.

87 The caricature could also depict composer and clarinet player Wim Poppink.

88 The photo by Boris Kowadlo is part of the Collectie Nederlands Fotomuseum Rotterdam and reprinted in Mehring (53).

89 Surprisingly, apart from well-known exceptions such as *Trees heeft een Canadees, Als op het Leidseplein de lichtjes weer eens branden gaan,* or *Lili Marleen,* few people remember songs such as *Vrij is Nederland, V-E Day, Herrijzend Nederland, Da-ag, Da-ag, Da-ag (How I like this way to say 'Hello'), Rotterdam Ahoy, Little Holland Girl, Eens zal de Wereld Zingen, Rood Wit Blauw, The Tommy Song, Tulips Bloom in Holland Once Again, Weet je Wat een Zoentje is?, Een Zoentje is 'A Little Kiss', or De 'Sten-Gun Walk'.* This remarkable gap in the history of liberation needs explaining.

90 Bulterman, *Snoezepoes*; emphases added by the author.

91 See Swart 226.

92 See Swart 227.

93 See Swart 233.

94 See Swart 232.

95 The Dutch original reads: 'We waren ook altijd op zoek naar goede nummers, waarin Kees de gelegenheid kreeg tot het spelen van zijn slagwerksoli. Zo ontstond bijvoorbeeld *Wie is Loesje*. Ik had over een drumnummer gedubd en een refreintje gevonden dat maar matig geschikt leek en ik had het daarom nog niet voor het orkest genoteerd. Er hoorde ook een couplet bij en daarvoor vond ik de woorden: "Wie is Loesje!" en bij impuls besefte ik dat dat het refrein moest zijn. "Wie is Loesje? Wie is toch dat snoesje?" En dan het hele orkest: "Loesje is 't meisje van de drummer van de band!" En verderop: "Hoor, daar slaat hij net een break!" (Djieng-boem, djieng-djieng-djieng-boem!) "Zij voelt in haar hart een steek!" (Pats!).' Quoted in de Kloet and de Wagt, *Mooi Holland?*, 70. Translation by the author.

96 A revealing case in point is an article in the *Gelderlander* newspaper from October 12, 1946 on the new film *Follies Girls* in the Scala Theater in Amsterdam. Its particular kind of jazz music and dancing is described as an attack on 'our good taste and partly also on our civiliza-

tion' ('aanslagen op onzen goeden smaak en ten deele, ook op onze beschaving'; 'Scala Theater' 2; translation by the author). Another derogative term used is 'Amerikaansche humbug' ('American humbug'; translation by the author). Acknowledging the positive aspects that the Americans have brought with the liberation, jazz however, ranked among the few exceptions which the Dutch allegedly could do without.

97 Information on the hit tune by The Ramblers is quite sparse and mentioned only in passing in Bulterman's *The Ramblers' Story* (1973) and de Kloet and de Wagt's *Mooi Holland?*.

98 See Morley 131.

99 The Dutch original reads: '*Bouncin' in Bavaria*, de van de AFN welbekende "tune", was een van de beste nummers van de avond'.

100 Other shows that catered to pop and jazz fans were *Rock and Roll Hop*, *Pop-Hitparade*, or *Jazz Album*. For an overview, see Rumpf, *Music in the Air* (116-18). See also Morley (133-35).

101 'Wer geglaubt hatte, mit den Amerikanern werde der Jazz Einzug in Deutschland halten, sah sich bald eines anderen belehrt, vor allem wenn er ein echter Jazzfan war. Er musste feststellen, dass der Durchschnittsamerikaner genauso viel und wenig vom Jazz wusste und sich dafür interessierte wie der Durchschnittsdeutsche. Die meisten Amerikaner bzw. U.S.-Soldaten hatten einen Hang zur Hill-Billy-(Cowboy-) Musik, zur Hawaiianmusik und billigsten Schlagern, vergleichbar etwa mit dem deutschen Faible für sentimentale 'Schnulzen(Schlager)' Musik und Heimatlieder. Im Allgemeinen galt jedoch alles als "Jazz", was von den diversen AFN (American Forces Network Soldatensender)-Stationen an amerikanischer Musik geboten wurde.'

102 Ate van Delden, vice president of the Dutch jazz magazine *Jazz Doctor*, points out that Armand Piron's New Orleans Orchestra recorded 'Bouncing Around' already in 1923 for Okeh Race Records. I am grateful for the reference.

103 Another reason can be tied to economic issues, since in postwar Germany it was difficult to forge a career on jazz beyond playing the familiar popular numbers of the past.

104 A competing orchestra from Germany, the Kurt Edelhagen Band was hailed as the 'best Band of the European Command' and recorded for AFN Munich during the same years as The Ramblers (Salaberger). While the U.S. occupational forces embraced Edelhagen's work and considered his orchestra 'Bigband No. 1' in the U.S. zone, Germans seemed more hesitant (Lange 155). The German magazine *Der Spiegel* suggested in 1952 that Edelhagen was more appreciated outside than inside Germany ('Edelhagen', 30). In Germany, Edelhagen's music was identified as 'healthy' reverting to Nazi categories, which distinguished German entertainment music from so-called 'degenerate' (*entartete*) music. There was no doubt that German jazz distinguished itself through absolute precision and hard work, implying that non-German jazz was part of light entertainment ('Edelhagen', 30). The article overemphasizes the (stereotypical) German work ethic Edelhagen allegedly had brought to jazz. Hence, according to the article, the artistry of German jazz was rooted not so much in American vitality but German perfection and dedication to hard work. By turning Edelhagen's music into an expression of Prussian values, jazz had become Germanized and, as the article implies, gained a distinction lacking in American productions.

105 The booklet received numerous reprints. It is estimated that it reached about 2.5 million Dutch people and was later translated to English to reach a larger audience beyond the Dutch nation. See Barry Machado, *In Search of a Usable Past: The MP and Postwar Reconstruction Today*. Lexington: George C. Marshall Foundation, 2007, 20. The booklet is available online

on the website of the Library of Congress, https://www.loc.gov/exhibits/marshall/mp1a.html

106 Translation by the author.

107 Similar wry humor underlies Jo Spier's cartoonish approach to the American aid program of the Marshall Plan.

108 Translation by the author.

109 Translation by the author.

110 Several Dutch bands recorded songs listed by Jan Hendriks on 78 shellac records. Among them were The Ramblers, directed by Theo Uden Masman, and The Skymasters, led by Pi Scheffer. The Kwartet or Orkest Jan Corduwener and the Kwintet Johnny Meijer also featured prominently, alongside The Millers with Sanny Day. Dick Willebrandts (en zijn) Radio-Orkest, Joop de Leur & McLinn, and The Moochers Septette made notable recordings as well. Additionally, the Internationals Dance Orchestra was among the groups whose recordings were among the songs that Hendriks played. I am grateful to Richard Piepenbrock from Nijmegen Blijft in Beeld for compiling this list.

111 Interview by the author and Anja Adriaans with Jan Hendriks in Nijmegen, reprinted in this book.

112 See e.g. a concert in the Freedom Museum under https:// www.ugenda.nl/home/nieuws/item/11599-jazz-en-dagboekfragmenten-uit-de-tweede-wereldoorlog

113 See Jan Hendriks. *Pianist in Bevrijdingstijd*. Nijmegen: Brakkenstein, 2004: 59.

114 The Twenty-One Club was set up by the Dutch military authorities. There was a ballot and a membership card. An advertisement in local newspaper *De Gelderlander* said that girls from good homes could register.

115 John Philip Sousa.

116 The Museum was then called National Liberation Museum 1944-1945.

117 Additionally, the persecution of LGBTQ+ individuals—referred to at the time simply as gay and lesbian relationships—highlights how love outside societal norms became particularly perilous during periods of upheaval, as explained in the museum's narrative. Simultaneously, the demand for transactional relationships surged, with a booming trade in 'love for sale' as people sought comfort and connection in uncertain times.

118 Translation by the author. The original is written in broken Dutch.

119 Unless noted differently, all translations by F. Mehring.

120 This list includes songs that were writing during the war but achieved a new meaning during and after the liberation (e.g. *Snoezepoes*) or popular songs that referred to the times of war and liberation (e.g. *De Trouwdag van Lili Marlene*). I am grateful to Hugo Keesing for tracing many of the liberation songs and freedom songs.

BIBLIOGRAPHY

Dutch Liberation Songs[120]

Als op het Leidseplein de lichtjes weer eens branden gaan. Words by Bert van Eijck, Music by Cor Steyn. G.J. van Zuylen, 1943.

America, We Thank You. Words by G. Bon and H. Joosen, Music by Louis Noiret. Amsterdam: Louis Noiret's Music Company, ca. 1949.

Amerika hat Rhythmus und Wien hat Melodie. Words by Erich Meder, English translation by Ezra Lapides, Music by Frank Fox. De Kruyff Doetinchem, 1945.

Arnhem Concerto. Dedicated to the Airbornes of 1944. Music by Felix Kwast. Marcanto, 1945.

The Bells Now Ring Again. Words and Music by Ar Colijn. A.v.d. Kleyn, 1945.

Bouncin' in Bavaria. Music by Jack Bulterman. Ch. Bens, 1948.

De Canadeesche Koorts. Words and Music by Jesse van de Weg, 1945.

Canuck-Song. Words and Music by Kees Sommer. Utrecht: J.H.A.H. Wagenaar, 1945.

Da-ag, Da-ag, Da-ag (How I like this way to say 'Hello'). Words and Music by Jack Bulterman. G.J. van Zuylen, 1945.

Dag Sjaan, dag Bep, dag Alida, De Groeten aan Amerika. Words by Fred Fagel and Marc Phail, Music by Tom Erich. C.W.H. Snoek, ca. 1945.

De Trouwdag van Lili Marlene (The Wedding of Lili Marlene). Lyrics and Music by Tommie Connor and Johnny Reine, Dutch words by Bart Ekkers. Amsterdam: Melodia, 1949.

Eens komt weer de dag van de VREDE! Words and Music by Willy Vervoort. Antwerpen: Schlager Editie, ca. 1945.

Eens zal de Wereld Zingen. Words by Han Dunk, Music by A. v.d. Ouderaa. C.W.H. Snoek, ca. 1940.

Gee, I like this Boogey Woogey Swing. Words by Bart Ekkers, Music by Han Ninaber. Roniepress, 1945.

Geef mij maar 'n echt Hollandsche Meisje. Words by Fred Fagel and Wim de Vries, Music by Fred Fagel, ca. 1945.

Goodbye Tommie Words by Arnold Frank, Music by Jean Evans. Antwerpen: Schlager Editie, 1945.

Herrijzend Nederland. Words by Anton Beuving, Music by Tom Erich. B.H. Smit, 1945.

Het Vrije Nederland. Words by Herre de Vos, Music by Johan Sluijter. Johitans, 1945.

De Hi Ha Holland Dans. Words and Music by Jaap de Bie. Metro Music Company, 1939.

Hokie Pokie (from Jimmy Kennedy's 'The Cokey Cokey'). B.H. Smit, 1942.

Holland, een Hymne. Words by E.J. Potgieter, Music by Ernest W. Mulder. H.J. Paris, 1942.

Ik kan niet swingen. Words by Bob Wallagh, Music by Fredy Salten. Basart, 1946.

I'll Be Seeing You (Jij zal bij mij zijn). Dutch words by Han Dunk, English words by Irving Kahal, Music by Sammy Fain. Metro Muziek, 1945.

Lili Marleen (Onder De Lantaren). Dutch Words by Arn. Frank, Music by N. Schultze. Gramac, 1939.

Little Holland Girl. Words and Music by Dutchie. Luctor, 1945.

Mamma, zijn naam is Johnny. Words and Music by Ar Colijn. A.v.d. Kleyn, 1945.

Mijn Holland. Words by Annie de Hoog-Nooy, Music by Joop de Leur. Amsterdam: B.H. Smit, 1945.

Mijn Tommy uit Canada. Words by Josef Baar, Music by Joop de Leur and Francis Bay. B.H. Smit, 1945.

Ons Holland is vrij. Words and Music by Fred Fagel. C.W.H. Snoek, 1945.

Sing Your Song of Thanks (to the Tommies and their Tanks). Words by T.C. Warrens, Music by Ar Colijn. A.v.d. Kleyn, 1945.

De Sten-Gun Walk. Words by Daan Hooykaas, Music by L. Fred Riks. C.W.H. Snoek, 1945.

Rood, Wit, Blauw. Music by Willy Schootemeyer. Hollanda, ca. 1939.

Rotterdam Ahoy. Words by Paul Duval, Music by Hans Ninaber. Edition Cosmopolite, 1945.

Rotterdams Glorie. Music by Jeronimus Hulsbergen. Rotterdam: Roniepers, 1945.

Snoezepoes. Words and Music by Jack Bulterman, German Lyrics by Hanns Kunz. The Hague: Muziek 'Smith', 1940/1945.

Thanks Tommies! Words and Music by Jack Bulterman. G.J. van Zuylen, 1945.

The Tommy Song. Words and Music by Kees Sommer. J.H.A.H. Wagenaar, 1945.

Trees heeft een Canadees. Words by Lou de Groot, Music by Albert de Booij. Roniepers, 1945.

De Trouwdag van Lili Marlene (The Wedding of Lili Marlene). Words and Music by Tommie Connor and Johnny Reine. Box & Cox Publications, 1949.

Tulips Bloom in Holland Once Again. Words and Music by William C. Blees. Dekeling & Swart, 1945.

V–E Day. Words by Anton Beuving, Music by Tom Erich. B.H. Smit, 1945.

Ver en Toch Nabij! (Just a Prayer Away). Words by Herre de Vos, Music by David Kapp. The Netherlands: B.H. Smit, 1944.

Vrede. Words by Clinge Doorenbos, Music by Jos Vranken. Van Zuylen, 1945.

Vrede voor Allen. Words and Music by Peter Lindeman. Amsterdam: G. Alsbach & Co., 1945.

Vredesmarsch. Music by Anton M. van Leest. V. Leest, 1945.

Vrij is Nederland (Jubelend Nederland #3). Words by Dico van der Meer, Music by Piet Lustenhouwer. Firma P. van Belkum Az., 194? [year missing].

De Vrijheidsmars. Words and Music by H.J. van Amersvoort. Muziekhandel H.J. van Amersvoort, ca. 1944.

Vrij is Nederland. Words by Dico van der Meer, Music by Piet Lustenhouwer. De Bilt, 1945.

Vry Nederland (Vryheidsmarsch). Words by Jan van Klooster, Music by Brucht van Klooster. Druk de Bussy, 1945.

Vrijheid en Recht. Words by Anton Beuving, Music by Tom Erich. B.H. Smit, 1945.

War is Over. Words and Music by Bill Buysman. B.H. Smit, Amsterdam, 1945.

We zijn weer Holland en we zijn weer vrij! Words and Music by Herman Stenz. G. Alsbach & Co., 1945.

Welcome Boy. Words by Arnold Frank, Music by Jean Evans. Antwerp: Muziek Uitgaven, 1945.

Wees Maar Gerust. Words by Han Dunk, Music by Gerhard Winkler. Metro-Muziek, 1943.

Weet je Wat een Zoentje is? Een Zoentje is 'A Little Kiss'. Words and Music by Herbert Nelson. The Netherlands: Metro Muziek, 1946.

Wij zijn weer vrij! (Lied van Vrijheid en Vrede). Words and Music by Herman Stenz. The Netherlands: G. Alsbach & Co., 1945.

Zij, die vielen..! Words by Anton Beuving, Music by Tom Erich. Amsterdam: B.H. Smit, ca. 1945.

Songs by Jack Bulterman

Bouncin' in Bavaria. Music by Jack Bulterman. Ch. Bens, 1948.

Clap your Hands and Twist. Words by Jack Bulterman, Music by Jack Bulterman and Bert Paige. Amsterdam: Editions 'Climax', 1962.

Da-ag, Da-ag, Da-ag (How I like this way to say 'Hello'). Words and Music by Jack Bulterman. G.J. van Zuylen, 1945.

Dag, Schatteboutje. Words and Music by Jack Bulterman. Amsterdam: Metro Muziek, n.d.

Dansmuziek/Tanzmusik. Dutch Words by Han Dunk, German Words by Hanns Kunz, Music by Jack Bulterman. Amsterdam: Metro Muziek, ca. 1931.

Hallo, Hella, Hallo. Words and Music by Jack Bulterman. Amsterdam: Edition Nagel, 1952.

Maa…rrr wij komen terug! Potpourri van de succesnummers, gespeeld door het dansorkest onder leiding van Theo Uden Masman, arrangement by Jack Bulterman. Amsterdam: Metro Muziek, n.d.

Morgen komt een nieuwe dag. Words by Maria Bartholomé and Music by Jack Bulterman. Brussel: Uitgave Ch. Bens, 1943.

Snoezepoes. Words and Music by Jack Bulterman. The Hague: Muziek 'Smith', 1940.

Swing me to Sleep, Drummer-man. Words and Music by Jack Bulterman. Amsterdam: ABC Muziek, date unknown.

Thanks Tommies! Words and Music by Jack Bulterman. G.J. van Zuylen, 1945.

Wie is Loesje? (Het Meisje van den Drummer van de Band). Words and Music by Jack Bulterman. Amsterdam: J. Poeltuyn, 1939.

Zuyderzee Blues. Words and Music by Jack Bulterman, arrangement by Jaap Meyer. The Hague: Muziek Smith, 1943.

American, British, and Canadian Songs of War and Liberation

Anna She Wears a Red Bandanna. Words and Music by William O. Rochow. William O. Rochow, 1944.

As Time Goes By. Words and Music by Herman Hupfeld. New York: Harms, 1931.

Basin Street Blues. Words and Music by Spencer Williams. New York: Mayfair Music Corp., 1933.

Blue Skies. Words and Music by Irving Berlin. New York: Irving Berlin, 1927.

Body and Soul. Words by Frank Eyton, Edward Heyman, Robert Sour, Music by John W. Green. New York: Harms, 1930.

The Chestnut Tree. Words and Music by Jimmy Kennedy, Tommie Connor, and Hamilton Kennedy. United Kingdom: Peter Maurice Music, 1939.

Convairina, Damsel from Douglas. Words and Music by O.B. and C.B. King. O.B. King, 1944.

Damsel from Douglas, The. Words and Music by Fethers. El Monte: Rich Publications, 1943.

Der Fuehrer's Face. Words and Music by Oliver Wallace. New York: Southern Music Publishing, 1942.

Dig Down Sister, The (Dig Down on the Farm). Words and Music by Lou Shelley, Allan Sage, and Karole Singer. Latin America Publishing Corp., 1943.

Farewell Blues. Words and Music by Leon Rappolo, Paul Mares, and Elmer Schoebel. New York: Jack Mills, 1923.

Fighting on the Home Front, WINS. Words and Music by Kay Swift. Chappell & Co., Inc., 1943.

Find the Cost of Freedom. Words and Music by Stephen Stills, 1970.

From the Old Swing Shift to the Kitchen. Words and Music by Dave Oppenheim and Ray Ingraham. Global Music Co., 1945.

Helping Her Honey Hurry Home. Words and Music by Eddie Alkire. Eddie Alkire, 1944.
How Will We Get Her Back in the Kitchen (After We've Won the War). Words and Music by Billy Hayes, Zeb Carver, and Jack Rollin. Peer International Corp., 1945.
I Can't Give You Anything But Love. Words by Jimmy McHugh, Music by Dorothy Fields and M. Kalua. New York: Jack Mills, 1928.
I'll Get By. Words by Roy Turk, Music by Fred E. Ahlert. New York: Irving Berlin, 1928 (Reprint 1943).
I'm in the Mood for Love. Words by Jimmy McHugh, Music by Dorothy Fields. New York: Robbins Music Corp., 1935.
In an Old Dutch Garden By an Old Dutch Mill. Words by Mack Gordon, Music by Will Grosz. New York: Harms, 1939.
In the Mood. Words and Music by Wingy Manone, Andy Razaf, and Joe Garland. New York: Shapiro, Bernstein & Co., 1939.
Lady's on the Job, The. Words and Music by Harold Rome. KayCee Music Co., Inc., 1943.
Let's Keep the Corsairs Flying High. Words and Music by John Fico and Lewis E. Faust. Hi-Tone Music Publishers, 1944.
Lili Marlene. Words by David Mack, Music by Norbert Schultze. New York: Chappell, 1943.
Lili Marlene. German Words by Hans Leip, English Words by Tommie Connor, Music by Norbert Schultze. New York: Edward B. Marks Music Corp., 1941, 1944.
Little Dutch Mill. Words by Ralph Freed, Music by Harry Barris. Select Music Publications, 1934.
Mama, Put Your Britches On. Words and Music by Irene Higginbotham. Beacon Music Company, 1943.
Man I Love, The. Words by Ira Gershwin, Music by George Gershwin. New York: Harms, 1924.
Marching and Singing! Words by Mark Minkus, Music by Henry Kane. New York: Patriotic Music Publishing Co., 1943.
Minnie's in the Money. Words and Music by Leo Robin and Harry Warren. Twentieth Century Music Corp., 1943.
Miss Victory. Words and Music by Fred Waring and Jack Dolph. Words and Music Inc., 1942.
My Gal's Working at Lockheed. Words and Music by Matt Dennis and Frank Loesser. Matt Dennis, 1941.
My Girl is a Regular Girl. Words and Music by Pvt. Milton Lustig and Milton Adair. Hamilton S. Gordon, Inc., 1943.
My Little W.O.W. Words and Music by Harold L.P. Johnson. Harold L.P. Johnson, 1943.
Mom's Building Bombers Now. Words and Music by Gladys Muhleman and J. Crane. Nordyke Publishing Co., 1945.
Mood Indigo. Words and Music by Duke Ellington, Irving Mills, and Barney Bigard. New York: Graham Music Service, 1931.
Old Glory: Star Spangled Rhythm. Words by Johnny Mercer, Music by Harold Arlen. New York: Famous Music Corporation, 1942.
Paper Doll. Words and Music by Johnny S. Black. New York: Shapiro, Bernstein & Co., Inc., 1921.
Plain Jane Doe. Words and Music by Sammy Cahn and Jule Styne. Paramount Music Corp., 1943.
Pluggin' Jane. Words and Music by Perry Alexander. Perry Alexander Music Publishing, 1943.
Praise the Lord and Pass the Ammunition! Words and Music by Frank Loesser. New York: Famous Music Corporation, 1942.
Remember Pearl Harbor. Words and Music by Don Reid and Sammy Kaye. New York: Republic Music, 1941.

Rise Up. Words and Music by Andra Day and Jennifer Decliveo, 2015.
Rosie the Riveter. Words and Music by John Loeb and Redd Evans. New York: Paramount Music, 1942.
She's that Airplane Working Baby of Mine. Words and Music by Don Moore. Don Moore, 1944.
Sweetheart in Overalls. Words and Music by Alfred Eiseman, Buddy Kaye, and Howard. Edwin H. Morris & Company, Inc., 1943.
Tea for Two. Words by Irving Caesar, Music by Vincent Youmans. New York: Harms, 1925.
Ten Little Soldiers. Words and Music by Abner Silver, Kay Werner, Sue Werner, Landt Trio and Curley. New York: Lincoln Music, 1942.
Tulips Are Talking Tonight, The. Words by Herb Magidson, Music by Jimmy McHugh. ABC Music Corporation, 1942.
Watch Your Step. Words and Music by Irving Berlin. New York: Irving Berlin, 1915.
We Did It Before. Words by Cliff Friend and Charlie Tobias. New York: M. Witmark & Sons, 1941.
We Shall Overcome. Origins unclear.
Wedding of Lili Marlene, The. Words and Music by Tommie Connor and Johnny Reine, Dutch Words by Bart Ekkers. Box & Cox, UK, 1949.
West End Blues. Music by Joe 'King' Oliver, 1928.
Worker in a War Plant, A. Words and Music by Albert Edward Freeman. Albert Edward Freeman, 1944.

Secondary Literature

Anderson, Benedict. *Imagined Communities: Reflections on the Origin and Spread of Nationalism*, rev. ed.. Verso, 2006.
Anonymous. 'De Gelderlander.' *De Gelderlander* [then *Arnhems dagblad*], May 5, 1945, p. 1.
Anonymous. 'Heiß vom Plattenteller.' *Der Spiegel*, Dec. 17, 1952, pp. 28–30.
Assmann, Aleida. *Cultural Memory and Western Civilization: Functions, Media, Archives*. Cambridge University Press, 2011.
Attali, Jacques. *Noise: The Political Economy of Music*. Translated by Brian Massumi. University of Minnesota Press, 1985.
Bak, Hans. 'On the Road to Nijmegen—Earle Birney and Alex Colville, 1944–1945.' *Politics and Cultures of Liberation: Media, Memory, and Projections of Democracy*, edited by Hans Bak, Frank Mehring, and Mathilde Roza. Brill, 2018, pp. 113–145.
Bergmeier, Horst J.P., and Rainer E. Lotz. *Hitler's Airwaves: The Inside Story of Nazi Radio Broadcasting and Propaganda Swing*. Yale University Press, 1997.
Bohländer, Carlo. 'The Evolution of Jazz Culture in Frankfurt: A Memoir.' *Jazz and the Germans: Essays on the Influence of 'Hot' American Idioms on the 20th Century German Music*, edited by Michael J. Budds. Pendragon Press, 2002, pp. 167–178.
Bolter, Jay David, and Richard Grusin. *Remediation: Understanding New Media*. MIT Press, 2000.
'Bounce.' *Oxford English Dictionary*, www.oed.com/.
Bulterman, Jack. *The Ramblers Story: 38 Jaar, Máárrr... Wij Komen Terug*. Van Holkema & Warendorf, 1973.
Connor, Walker. *Ethnonationalism: The Quest for Understanding*. Princeton University Press, 1994.
Cooke, Mervyn. *A History of Film Music*. Cambridge University Press, 2008.
Craig, R. Stephen. 'The American Forces Network, Europe: A Case Study in Military Broadcasting.' *Journal of Broadcasting & Electronic Media*, vol. 30, no. 1, 1968, pp. 33–46.

——. 'Medium-wave Frequency Allocations in Postwar Europe: U.S. Foreign Policy and the Copenhagen Conference of 1948.' *Journal of Broadcasting & Electronic Media,* vol. 34, no. 2, 1990, pp. 119–135.

Donkers, Jan. *De Amerikaanse Droom in Nederland 1944–1969.* Uitgeverij SUN, 2000.

Edelhagen, Kurt. 'Präzis wie die Preußen.' *Der Spiegel,* Oct. 27, 1952, pp. 27–30.

Eichenauer, Richard. *Musik und Rasse.* Lehmann, 1932.

Filene, Benjamin. *Romancing the Folk: Public Memory & American Roots Music.* University of North Carolina Press, 2000.

Flannery-McCoy, Christopher. 'Analysis and History of Major Choral Arrangements of "We Shall Overcome".' *We Shall Overcome: Essays on a Great American Song,* edited by Victor V. Bobetsky. Rowman & Littlefield, 2015, pp. 59–76.

Floyed, Samuel. *The Power of Black Music: Interpreting Its History from Africa to the United States.* Oxford University Press, 1995.

Fluck, Winfried. *Romance with America? Essays on Culture, Literature, and American Studies,* edited by Laura Bieger and Johannes Voelz. Heidelberg: Universitätsverlag Winter, 2009.

Frank, Anne. *The Diary of a Young Girl: The Definitive Edition.* Doubleday, 1995.

Gerhard, Paul, and Ralph Schock, eds. *Sound des Jahrhunderts: Geräusche, Töne, Stimmen 1889 bis heute.* Bundeszentrale für politische Bildung, 2013.

Gilmour, Michael J. *The Gospel According to Bob Dylan: The Old, Old Story for Modern Times.* Westminster John Knox Press, 2011.

Groeneveld, Gerard. *Zo zong de NSB: Liedcultuur van de NSB 1931–1945.* Uitgeverij Vantilt, 2007.

Grosz, Wilhelm, and Mack Gordon. 'In an Old Dutch Garden (by an Old Dutch Mill).' New York, 1939.

Havinga, Rense. 'De Soundtrack van de Bevrijding Tentoonstellen.' *Soundtrack van de Bevrijding: Swingen, Zingen en Dansen op Weg Naar Vrijheid,* edited by Frank Mehring. Uitgeverij Vantilt, 2015, pp. 102–108.

Hebel, Udo J. 'American Pictures and (Trans-)National Iconographies: Mapping Interpictorial Clusters in American Studies.' *Journal of Transnational American Studies,* vol. 6, no. 1, 2015, pp. 401–431.

Heister, Hanns-Werner. 'Politische Musik.' *Die Musik in Geschichte und Gegenwart,* vol. 7, 1997, pp. 1661–1682.

Hendriks, Jan. *Pianist in Bevrijdingstijd.* Brakkenstein, 2004.

Historie. *The Ramblers.* Stichting The Ramblers, n.d., Web.

Hoppe, Joseph. 'AFN Berlin: 'Frolic at Five'—Mehr als ein Soldatensender.' *Coca-Cola, Jazz und AFN: Berlin und die Amerikaner,* edited by Tamara Domentat, Schwarzkopf und Schwarzkopf, 1995, pp. 118–127.

Horn, Michail. 'More Than Cigarettes, Sex and Chocolate: The Canadian Army in the Netherlands, 1944–1945.' *Journal of Canadian Studies / Revue des Études Canadiennes,* vol. 16, no. 3, Fall 1981, pp. 156–173.

Hornung, Alfred, and Rüdiger Kunow. 'Preface to Global Fictions.' *Amerikastudien / American Studies,* vol. 47, no. 2, 2002, pp. 193–198.

Huijnen, Pim, and Jaap Verheul. 'Reference Cultures and Imagined Empires in Western History: Global Perspectives, 1815–2000.' *CFP,* Utrecht University, June 11–13, 2014, Web.

Jacobs, Annelies. *Het geluid van gisteren. Waarom Amsterdam vroeger ook niet stil was.* Universitaire Pers Maastricht, 2014.

Jacobs, Annelies, and Karin Bijsterveld. 'Der Klang der Besatzungszeit: Amsterdam 1940 bis 1945.' *Sound des Jahrhunderts: Geräusche, Töne, Stimmen 1889 bis heute*, edited by Gerhard Paul and Ralph Schock, Bundeszentrale für politische Bildung, 2013, pp. 252–257.

Kater, Michael H. *Different Drummers: Jazz in the Culture of Nazi Germany.* Oxford University Press, 1992.

Kaufman, Gerhard. *Orgel und Nationalsozialismus: Die ideologische Vereinnahmung des Instrumentes im 'Dritten Reich.'* Musikwissenschaftliche Verlagsgesellschaft, 1997.

Keesing, Hugo. *Youth in Transition: A Content Analysis of Two Decades of Popular Music.* Diss. Adelphi University, 1972.

Kloet, Co de, and Gabri de Wagt. *Mooi Holland? De Woelige Jaren van de Ramblers.* Heuff, 1981.

Koopes, Enne. *De Dynamiek van een Emigratiecultuur: De emigratie van gereformeerden, hervormden en katholieken naar Noord-Amerika in vergelijkend perspectief (1947–1963).* Uitgeverij Verloren, 2010.

Lange, Horst H. *Jazz in Deutschland: Die deutsche Jazz-Chronik 1900–1966.* Olms, 1966.

Leur, Walter van de. 'Pure Jazz and Charlatanry: A History of De Jazzwereld Magazine, 1931–1940.' *Current Research in Jazz,* vol. 4, 2012.

——. 'The Reception and Development of Jazz in the Netherlands (1945–1970s).' *Politics and Cultures of Liberation: Media, Memory, and Projections of Democracy*, edited by Hans Bak, Frank Mehring, and Mathilde Roza. Brill, 2018, pp. 177–191.

Machado, Barry. *In Search of a Usable Past: The MP and Postwar Reconstruction Today.* George C. Marshall Foundation, 2007.

MacLean, Fitzroy. *Escape to Adventure*. Boston: Little, Brown & Co., 1950.

Magee, Jeffrey. *Irving Berlin's American Musical Theater.* Oxford University Press, 2012.

Mehring, Frank. 'Liberation Songs: Music and the Cultural Memory of the Dutch Summer of 1945.' *Politics and Cultures of Liberation: Media, Memory, and Projections of Democracy*, edited by Hans Bak, Frank Mehring, and Mathilde Roza. Brill, 2018, pp. 149–176.

——. 'Meditating and Broadcasting the Lingua Franca of Jazz in Postwar Germany and the Netherlands.' *JIPSS—Journal for Intelligence, Propaganda and Security Studies,* vol. 17, no. 1, 2023, pp. 27–41.

——. 'Only a Pawn in Their Game? Civil Rights Sounding Signatures in the Summer of 1963.' *Sonic Politics: Music and Social Movements in the Americas*, edited by Olaf Kaltmeier and Wilfried Raussert. Routledge, 2019, pp. 51–72.

——. 'Rosies Across Ideologies: Intermedial and Transnational Approaches to an American Female Icon.' *Women and U.S. Politics: Historical and Contemporary Perspectives: Essays in Honor of Hans-Juergen Grabbe*, edited by Julia Nitz and Axel R. Schaefer. Winter Verlag, 2020, pp. 103–124.

——. *Sphere Melodies: Die Manifestation Transzendentalistischer Ideen in der Musik von Charles Ives und John Cage.* Metzler, 2003.

——. *De Soundtrack van de Bevrijding: Swingen, Zingen en Dansen op Weg naar Vrijheid.* With contributions by Anja Adriaans, Jens Barnieck, Rense Havinga, and Hugo Keesing. Uitgeverij Vantilt, 2015.

——. 'You Too Can Be Like Us! Friendly Persuasion, Self-Americanization, and the Utopia of a New Europe.' *Selling Democracy / Friendly Persuasion*, edited by Rainer Rother, DHM, 2006, pp. 35–46.

Mehring, Frank, and Jaap Verheul, eds. *Faces of Liberation.* Amsterdam University Press, 2025.

Mitchell, W.J.T. *What Do Pictures Want? The Lives and Loves of Images.* University of Chicago Press, 2005.
Mitry, Jean. *The Aesthetics and Psychology of the Cinema.* Indiana University Press, 1997.
Morley, Patrick. *This Is the American Forces Network: The Anglo-American Battle of the Air Waves in World War II.* Praeger, 2001.
Mutsaers, Lutgard. *Beat Crazy: Een Pophistorisch Onderzoek naar de Impact van de Transnationale Dansrages Twist, Disco en House in Nederland.* EML Books, 1998.
Nye, Joseph. *The Future of Power.* PublicAffairs, 2011.
Oudejans, Frans. 'Jacques Cornelis Bulterman (1909–1977).' *Biografisch Woordenboek Van Nederland,* vol. 3, The Hague, 1989.
Phleps, Thomas. 'Musik und Ideologie.' *Musikpsychologie: Ein Handbuch*, edited by Herbert Bruhn et al. Rowohlt Taschenbuch, 2002, pp. 94–103.
Polster, Bernd, ed. *Swing Heil! Jazz im Nationalsozialismus.* Transit, 1989.
Pratt, Mary Louise. 'The Arts of the Contact Zone.' *Profession 91,* 1991, pp. 33–40.
Raussert, Wilfried, and James Miller Jones, eds. *Travelling Sounds: Music, Migration, and Identity in the U.S. and Beyond.* LIT Verlag, 2008.
Rumpf, Wolfgang. *Music in the Air: AFN, BEBS, OE3, Radio Luxemburg und die Radiokultur in Deutschland.* LIT Verlag, 2007.
——. 'Music in the Air: AFN: Neue Musik, Neue Radiokultur, Neues Lebensgefühl.' *Sound des Jahrhunderts: Geräusche, Töne, Stimmen 1889 bis heute*, edited by Gerhard Paul and Ralph Schock, Bundeszentrale für politische Bildung, 2013.
Salaberger, Gerd. 'Ein Streiter für den Jazz: Gespräche mit Kurt Edelhagen.' *Frankfurter Rundschau,* July 14, 1949, p. 8.
Scala Theater. 'Follies Girl.' *De Gelderlander,* Oct. 12, 1940, p. 2.
Schafer, R. Murray. *The Thinking Ear: Complete Writings on Music Education.* Arcana Editions, 1986.
Schäfers, Anja. *Mehr als Rock 'n' Roll: Der Radiosender AFN bis Mitte der sechziger Jahre.* Franz Steiner Verlag, 2014.
Sierp, Aline. 'Integrating Europe, Integrating Memories: The EU's Politics of Memory since 1945.' *The Transcultural Turn: Interrogating Memory Between and Beyond Borders*, edited by Lucy Bond and Jessica Rapson. De Gruyter, 2014, pp. 103–118.
Smith, Kathleen E.R. *God Bless America: Tin Pan Alley Goes to War.* University Press of Kentucky, 2003.
Southern, Eileen. *The Music of Black Americans: A History.* 3rd ed. Norton & Company, 1997.
Spier, Jo. *Het Marshall Plan en U.* De Persdienst van het Ministerie van Economische Zaken, 1949.
Sterne, Jonathan. *The Audible Past: Cultural Origins of Sound Reproduction.* Duke University Press, 2003.
——, ed. *The Sound Studies Reader.* Routledge, 2012.
Strößner, Gerhard. 'Der Aufbau von AFN in Nordbayern.' *Kleeblatt Radio,* vol. 2, 1992, 22.
Swart, Aat. 'Popular and Light Music.' *Music in Holland: A Review of Contemporary Music in the Netherlands*, edited by Eduard Reeser. J.M. Meulenhoff, 1959, pp. 223–235.
Uricchio, William. 'Things to Come in the American Studies–Media Studies Relationship.' *American Studies Today: New Research Agendas*, edited by Winfried Fluck, Erik Redling, Sabine Sielke, and Hubert Zapf. Universitätsverlag Winter, 2014, pp. 363–382.
Wagnleitner, Reinhold. *Coca-Colonization and the Cold War: The Cultural Mission of the United*

States in Austria after the Second World War, University of North Carolina Press, 1994.
——. 'Jazz—The Classical Music of Globalization.' *Travelling Sounds: Music, Migration, and Identity in the U.S. and Beyond*, edited by Wilfried Raussert and James Miller Jones. LIT Verlag, 2008, pp. 23–60.
Ward, Brian. 'Sounds and Silences: Music and the March on Washington.' *Staging a Dream: Untold Stories and Transatlantic Legacies of the March on Washington*, edited by Britta Waldschmidt-Nelson, Marcia Chatelain, and Sharon Monteith. *Bulletin of the German Historical Institute,* 2015, pp. 25–48.
Weizsäcker, Richard von. 'Gedenkveranstaltung im Plenarsaal des Deutschen Bundestages zum 40. Jahrestag des Endes des Zweiten Weltkrieges in Europa.' *Bundestag, Bonn,* May 8, 1985, Bundespräsident. Bundespräsidialamt, https://www.bundespraesident.de/SharedDocs/Reden/DE/Richard-von-Weizsaecker/Reden/1985/05/19850508_Rede.html
Willett, Ralph. *The Americanization of Germany 1945–1949*. Routledge, 1989.
Wouters, Kees. 'The Introduction of Jazz in The Netherlands.' *Four Centuries of Dutch-American Relations 1609–2009*, edited by Hans Krabbendam, Cornelis A. van Minnen, and Giles Scott-Smith. Boom, 2009, pp. 497–508.
---. 'Fear of the "Uncivilised": Dutch Responses to American Entertainment Music, 1920–1945.' *American Culture in the Netherlands*, edited by Doeko Bosscher, Marja Roholl, and Mel van Elteren. VU University Press, 1996, pp. 43–61.
Zwerin, Mike. *La Tristesse de Saint Louis: Swing under the Nazis.* Morrow, 1985.

LIST OF CONTRIBUTORS

Anja Adriaans graduated cum laude from North American Studies at Radboud University Nijmegen. She cooperated in the book *The Crossing. A Dutch Tribute to 48 American War Heroes*. During this work she uncovered the humanitarian involvement of the U.S. Army in rebuilding Nijmegen after WWII. She is founder/director of the FAN: Friendship Albany NY & Nijmegen foundation that rekindles the post-WWII 'sister cities' friendship between Nijmegen and Albany, NY that followed from the 1947 aid campaign. Adriaans is an Honorary Member of the 504th Parachute Infantry Regiment of the 82nd Airborne Division, Fort Bragg, NC.

Dean Burry is a Toronto-based librettist, composer, and educator. Burry has written twelve nationally and internationally performed theatrical works for young people, including *The Hobbit*, *The Secret World of Og*, *The Scorpions' Sting*, *The Bremen Town Musicians*, *Le nez de la sorcière*, *The Vinland Traveler*, *Angela and Her Sisters*, *Pandora's Locker*, and *The Sword in the Schoolyard*. His opera *The Brothers Grimm*, commissioned by the Canadian Opera Company in 1999, has been presented over 600 times and is considered 'the most performed Canadian opera in history' (Bill Richardson, CBC's Saturday Afternoon at the Opera). He is also a professor of new and Canadian music at the Glenn Gould Professional School of the Royal Conservatory. Burry was the 2011 recipient of the Ontario Arts Foundation's Louis Applebaum Composers Award for excellence in the field of music for young people.

Jens Barnieck is an internationally active pianist, with world premier recordings of the piano works of Friedrich Gernsheim (Toccata Classics) and works by Joseph Bologne, Chevalier de Saint-George (Coviello Records). He studied at Music University Detmold and State University of New

York at Buffalo. Sponsorships: Bundeskulturstiftung/Land Hessen (Cité Internationale des Arts, Paris and German Study Center Venice), German Music Foundation, Avenira Foundation Switzerland, Hessische Kulturstiftung, KulturFonds Frankfurt Rhein Main, Schiedmayer-Stiftung; Artist-in-Residence at the Virginia Center for the Creative Arts. www.jensbarnieck.de

Rense Havinga received his MA in Military History and Military Science from the University of Amsterdam in 2010. He has been working as curator and head of exhibitions at the Freedom Museum in Groesbeek, the Netherlands since 2011. He led the team that created the permanent exhibition of the Freedom Museum in 2019 and has produced seventeen temporary exhibitions, among them 'Songs of Liberation' (2015). Author of *De Zwarte Driehoek. De geschiedenis van als 'asociaal' vervolgden 1933–1945* (Amsterdam, 2022).

Hugo Keesing, retired adjunct associate professor American Studies, University of Maryland, has been researching the role and function of music in wartime for more than 50 years. His personal collection of some 11,000 pieces of World War II sheet music includes many of the examples in this book related to Holland's liberation. He is the reissue producer and author of 'Battleground Korea—Songs and Sounds of America's Forgotten War', a 4-CD, 160-page book 'boxed set' that received a 2018 Grammy nomination for Best Historical Album.

Frank Mehring is Professor of American Studies at Radboud University, Nijmegen. His research explores cultural transfer, migration, intermediality, and the role of music in transnational contexts. His notable publications include *Sphere Melodies* (2003), which examines the intersection of literature and music in the works of Charles Ives and John Cage, and *Sound and Vision: Intermediality and American Music* (2018, co-authored with Erik Redling). Mehring has uncovered a significant visual archive of transatlantic modernism, contributing articles, lectures, exhibitions, editions, and catalogs such as *The Multicultural Modernism of Winold Reiss* (2022). He also organized the first performance of the Marshall Plan opera *La Sterlina Dollarosa* (2018) and together with pianist Jens Barnieck recorded and produced music videos of liberation songs for the 2020 Canadian Tulip Festival.

Jo Riding is currently the Executive Director of the Canadian Tulip Festival. With an education in Film, Media and Scriptwriting, she founded and ran a top-rated Film Production Company in Toronto for 10 years, and then an award-winning Multimedia Marketing Agency in Ottawa for another decade. Riding has also received a Hot Docs Award as Documentary Producer and many prizes as Music Video Producer. Most recently she received the World Tulip Summit Award for Best Commemorative Entertainment at the Canadian Tulip Festival. Storytelling through film, television, social media, interactive events, galas, trade shows, and festivals for the last 30 years, Riding has joyfully entertained millions of Canadians and successfully hosted hundreds of thousands of guests from across the globe.

Mooi Holland, cover (1945)

INDEX OF PERSONS

Acuff, Roy 108
Alexander, Perry 67
Anderson, Lale (Lieselotte Helene Berta Bunnenberg) 62
Armstrong, Louis Daniel 96, 130, 237
Astaire, Fred 235
Attali, Jacques 17, 18, 30, 35, 233
Baez, Joan 16
Bandy, Lou 114, 133
Beethoven, Ludwig van 59
Bechet, Sidney Joseph 91, 237
Beek, Hendrik van 50, 52
Bertelmann, Volker 36
Berlin, Irving (Israel Beilin) 110
Birney, Earle 84, 171, 236
Bizet, Georges 111
Blees, William C. 116
Bon, G. 167, 208
Booy, Albert de 169
Bouvet, Jean 65
Brinitzer, Carl 59, 235
Calloway, Cabell "Cab" 96
Castle, Irene Foote 71
Castle, Vernon (Vernon Blythe) 71
Colijn, Ar 50, 112
Colville, Alex 23, 161-165, 232, 236
Crosby, Bing (Harry Lillis Crosby Jr.) 29, 59, 99
Crosby, David Van Cortlandt 16, 171
Dabney, Ford Thompson 71
Day, Andra (Cassandra Monique Batie) 18

Day, Doris Mary Anne Kappelhoff 29
Desplat, Alexandre Michel Gérard 36
Dietrich, Marlene (Marie Magdalene Dietrich) 62, 63, 65, 235
Dorsey, Jimmy (James Francis Dorsey) 29
Dorsey, Tommy (Thomas Francis Dorsey Jr.) 86, 159
Dunk, Han 57, 166, 175, 177
Dylan, Bob (Robert Allen Zimmerman) 16, 153, 173, 232
Eisenhower, Dwight David 152, 188
Eichenauer, Richard 44
Ekkers, Bart 62, 235
Ellington, Edward Kennedy "Duke" 21, 26, 90, 92, 96, 126, 130, 237
Erich, Tom 19, 55
Europe, James Reese 71
Evans, Redd (Walter Evans) 66, 235
Fitzroy, Maclean 62
Fox, Frank 167
Frank, Anne (Annelies Marie Frank) unpaginated
Friedhofer, Hugo Wilhelm 36
Friedriks, Leo (Fred Riks) 77
Foulkes, Charles 168
Gaga, Lady (Stefani Joanne Angelina Germanotta) 18
Gillespie, Dizzy 237
Goebbels, Joseph 59, 237
Goodman, Benny (Benjamin David Goodman) 90, 106
Gonella, Nathaniel Charles "Nat" 106
Gounod, Charles-François 111
Griffith, David Wark (D.W.) 36
Groot, Lou de 167, 222, 243
Hawkins, Coleman Randolph 98
Haydn, Franz Joseph 164
Hendriks, Jan 20, 21, 83, 120-126, 128, 131, 132, 237, 240
Hindemith, Paul 37, 91
Himmler, Heinrich 44
Hitler, Adolf 42, 59, 70, 82, 189, 191, 237
Hooykaas, Daan 167, 192, 193
Ives, Charles Edward 37, 233
Joosten, H. 167, 208
Jones, Grandpa (Louis Marshall Jones) 108
Kenswil, Atma 166, 179, 180
Kranenburg, Kees 91
Kranenburg, Ph.M. 167
Kracauer, Siegfried 35
Krenek, Ernst 37, 91
Kubik, Gail Thompson 36
Kunz, Hanns 99, 241, 242
Kwast, Felix 166, 181, 182
Lapides, Ezra 167, 182, 199
Leip, Hans 59, 60, 163, 182
Leoncavallo, Ruggero 111
Loeb, John Jacob 66, 235
London Five 96
Lynn, Vera Margaret Welch 29, 158, 159, 162, 227
Maclean, Fitzroy Hew Royle 62, 234

Marleen, Lili 20, 33, 57, 59, 60, 62, 63, 65, 163, 166, 182-184, 234, 238
Marshall, George Catlett 32, 112-114, 116, 208-210, 233, 236
Masman, Theo Uden 91, 103, 237
Meder, Erich 167, 199, 200
Millar, Jack 71, 99
Miller, Glenn 29, 31, 59, 86, 88, 89, 99, 108, 110, 112, 158, 159
Mitry, Jean 35, 234
Montgomery, Bernard Law 188
Mozart, Wolfgang Amadeus 164
Mueller-Blattau, Joseph 44
Mussolini, Benito Amilcare Andrea 42
Nash, Graham William 16, 171
Ninaber, Hans 88
Nixon, Richard Milhous 154
Noiret, Louis 167, 208
Original Victoria Band 96
Parker, Charlie (Charles Parker Jr) 111
Parker, Nate 18
Patton, George Smith Jr 188
Platters, The 152, 153
Porter, Cole Albert 121, 132
Puccini, Giacomo Antonio Domenico Michele Secondo Maria 111
Ramblers, The 72, 91, 92, 95, 96, 98, 103, 106, 107, 109, 112, 114, 118, 120, 131, 196, 197, 221, 235, 237-240
Reese, James 71
Renden, Barend 167, 212, 213
Riot, Pussy 17, 18, 232
Rockwell, Norman Perceval 70
Ruesing, Bernd 65
Salter, Fredy 167, 203
Schultze, Norbert 59, 62, 166, 182, 184-186
Schulhoff, Erwin 91
Seeger, Pete (Peter Seeger) 16
Seyffardt, H.A. 45
Thielemans, Jean-Baptiste Frédéric Isidor Marcel “Toots” 92
Toscanini, Arturo 37
Verschuur, Nelly 57, 175
Verdi, Giuseppe Fortunino Francesco 111
Whiteman, Paul Samuel 91, 97
Young, Neil Percival 16, 171
Young, Victor 36
Zom, Pierre Jr. 77, 192